THE

OFF

SWITCH

THE OFF SWITCH

SWITCH

Leave work on time
relax your mind
but still get more done

PROFESSOR MARK CROPLEY

1 3 5 7 9 10 8 6 4 2

Virgin Books, an imprint of Ebury Publishing,
20 Vauxhall Bridge Road,
London SW1V 2SA

Virgin Books is part of the Penguin Random House group of companies
whose addresses can be found at global.penguinrandomhouse.com

Penguin
Random House
UK

First published in The United Kingdom by Virgin Books in 2015

www.eburypublishing.co.uk

A CIP catalogue record for this book is available from the British Library

ISBN: 9780753556696

Printed and bound by Clay Ltd, St Ives, Plc

FSC
www.fsc.org
MIX
Paper from
responsible sources
FSC® C018179

Contents

Foreword

One evening a few years ago I was sitting in a pub waiting for some friends when I overheard two women talking at a nearby table. I can't remember exactly what they looked like — both were in their mid-forties — or exactly what they were saying, but I can recall the gist of their conversation and certain words they used. The general topic of their conversation, as it invariably is when people socialise, was to do with work. One of the women was bemoaning the fact that she couldn't leave work behind, she could never 'escape' from work and that work-related thoughts consumed all her waking hours. I never found out, although I was tempted to ask, what she did for a living, though I figured she was probably an accountant or an office manager.

As the conversation developed, she said that it got worse during the evenings. She said that at night, as she was lying in bed, her mind kept 'churning and churning' and was unable to stop. I thought this was an excellent way of describing her thought processes and I have come across many individuals who experience the same problem. Instead of being able to switch off at the end of the day, many find their work-related thoughts accompany them on their journeys home and continue to bother them during their leisure time. One remedy people adopt is simply to carry on working when they get home. This is all too easy today with electronic devices that allow for instant messaging and constant contact with work. We now know that, if left unchecked, this style of thinking is very bad for our health, wellbeing and sanity.

There is an alternative. The aim of this book is to help people like the woman in the pub and others to let go and turn off the metaphorical switch that connects them to their work but nonetheless still allow them to be successful and productive in their careers. People who are able to switch off and unwind at the end of the working day are also much happier and healthier, and they also tend to get more done at work.

In the current economic climate and with the extra demands we all face at work in order for our companies to be successful, you may think it's a little outrageous to write a book about not working and not thinking about work. However, I can assure you it's not that crazy and the two are not incompatible. In fact, rest and recreation, and engaging in leisure pursuits, are just as vital to work as work itself, and people who work 'normal' hours can be much more productive and creative than overcommitted workers.

There are innumerable self-help books on the market and many of these offer sound, practical advice on ways to cope with occupational stress. There is a clear need for these types of books. What has become apparent over the last few years, however, is that it is not necessarily the amount of stress one experiences at work that is the cause of ill health, but it is how quickly one is able to recover once the actual stressor (the thing that's making you feel stressed) has passed. Failure to unwind successfully after work is therefore a major health concern. It is now thought that the speed of recovery may be more important in the development of disease and illness than the acute response during the period of stress. There is also overwhelming evidence that working too much, and failing to unwind, is associated with reduced productivity, poor decision-making, poor creativity and increased risk of engaging in deviant behaviour in the workplace. Thus, more than ever before, there is a clear need for all of us to take time to unwind and relax post-work.

Different people need different amounts of time to unwind and 'switch off' from work during their leisure time and a high percentage of workers find it difficult to recover from the effects of work post-work. This book introduces the reader to techniques/exercises that have been found to help people to 'switch off' from work-related thoughts. It is aimed at a general audience, and it is not meant to be an authoritative text on stress or unwinding from work. Unfortunately there is no one model fits all remedy; I do not have the answers for everyone. Each person appears to have their own inimitable way of relaxing and unwinding, but the following chapters offer a guided tour through the research that I and others have conducted.

Lifestyle plays an important role in most illnesses and disease, and lifestyle is the main contributing factor to successfully unwinding and recovering from the effects of work. Often when we are extremely busy we become like the proverbial rabbit caught in the headlights — we don't know which way to turn and how to effect change. We need to take stock of the situation, and then take remedial action. In theory, the first principle in any remedial process is to identify the cause of the problem; the second is to remove the cause; the third is to reduce the symptoms; and the fourth is to gain strength to develop resilience in order to prevent the problem reoccurring. With this principle in mind, I have arranged the book into four sections. Part I discusses why it is important to unwind and switch off from work but still get more done. Part II introduces chapters on how to deal with work-related thoughts when not at work, and how to take control of your life. This part is concerned with removing the causes of why you can't unwind during your leisure time. Part III examines ways of removing the cause of poor unwinding from the perspective of the working day; that is, what you can do during the working day to improve how you unwind during the evening. By following the advice and exercises in Parts II and III, you will develop a number of unwinding techniques and ameliorate your response to unwinding. In Part IV, I offer ways in which you can develop resilience and how to respond when the going gets tough.

Many chapters include real-life case studies. The individuals concerned are people my colleagues and I have interviewed, and we report the methods they have found useful. All names have been changed to maintain anonymity. We need to think actively about how we switch off from work in order to enjoy our free time, to protect our health, have more energy, sleep better, so that we get more done the next day. There is no easy quick fix, and while these methods will require practice none of the exercises are too arduous. One thing I can guarantee is that if you follow the advice I offer in this book you will not only feel more in control of your life, you will also become healthier, fitter and more productive than you have ever been.

Happy unwinding!

Thinking about work and why it's important to relax the mind

Overview

There are no short cuts to having a successful career. Most people who succeed work extremely hard. Unfortunately, hard work and long hours do not always equate to productivity, and hard work does not necessarily guarantee success. We need to focus at work to be productive and successful but we also need time to unwind and reflect so we don't become stale. Successful people work hard and enjoy their work but they also know when and how to relax and appreciate other things life has to offer. As with most aspects of life, it is a question of balance. Too much work is not good for us; nor is too much rest.

As an intelligent species you would think we would easily spot when we are pushing ourselves too much. For some peculiar reason, however, our minds and bodies have developed a strange way of adjusting to the demands we place on them. In many cases we just don't notice we are spending a little longer in the office, or taking a little extra work home — just to finish off after dinner — as work gradually creeps up on us. We become easily accustomed to the way of life, and push even more, and we may not even realise how fatigued or exhausted we are. We can become so consumed by work or thinking about work that we don't know we are developing the early signs of burnout until it is too late. It is as if we are oblivious to any signals that we are in trouble. We may not even realise we have been pushing ourselves too much until the day it hits us.

Rather than allow you to reach this point, the aim of the first part of the book is to encourage you to take stock, and think about what you are actually doing in your working life. The aim of Part I is to get you to start thinking about work not simply in terms of how many hours you put in, but also to think about the mental energy you invest in work even when you are not at work. To my mind, if you are thinking about work even during your leisure time, this is still work. Therefore you need to find time and ways to relax the mind. To this end, this first part lays the foundations for the remainder of the book, and discusses the joys of working; it also highlights the dangers to health of overworking and why it's fundamentally important to find time to unwind and escape from work. As you will see in chapters 1 to 4, striking the right balance between work and rest has clear benefits for both the employee and the employer.

In order to be productive and successful in our goals we need to arrive at work feeling refreshed and energised. This is less likely to happen if we don't find time to unwind and switch off during our free time. In chapter 5 of this part I present a way of assessing how you think about work outside work and here I have included a measure to assess 'your own off switch'.

1
All work and no play

'Fie upon this quiet life! I want work'

William Shakespeare, *Henry IV, Part 1*

Jessica

Jessica was a fifty-two-year-old mother of two grown-up daughters and a self-employed bookkeeper. She came to see me as she said that she could never escape from work. Jessica has always been a hard worker, and was brought up with a strong work ethic; perhaps because of this, at eighteen she went straight into work instead of going to university. She started out as a general administrator, but somewhere along the way she was asked to help with the company accounts where she was working and started bookkeeping. This was something she enjoyed but she never took the time to sit the required exams; she thought she had too much work to complete, and would be letting her boss down if she didn't work late most evenings. She had even pulled all-nighters when there were important deadlines. She thought her commitment would be warmly received by senior management, but when restructuring 'was forced' within the company, it was decided that Jessica did not have the appropriate qualifications needed to take the company forward.

Being made redundant hit Jessica hard, and it took her a while to pull herself together. Because of her lack of formal qualifications in accountancy many jobs were not open to her, even though she clearly had the skills and knowledge to do the work. However, after a chance meeting with a friend who was struggling to get his tax returns in, she offered to help. Gradually word spread, and more and more people began asking her to keep their books. Within a few months the work started to pour in. Her clients are mainly self-employed people, most working in the building industry: bricklayers, plumbers, plasterers, etc.

One of Jessica's problems – arguably her main problem – is knowing when her work is done, and worrying that she could have done more. Due to the insecurity of being self-employed, Jessica has difficulty turning away work, as, in her words, 'you don't know what is around the corner'. Rarely does she turn work away and consequently, she works extremely long hours in order to complete the work.

When Jessica came to see me, she was showing clear signs of the beginnings of chronic fatigue. She said that she was constantly tired, unfit and overweight, and at a loss as to what to do. She knew that she needed to react before her life got completely out of control and she knew she was at risk of developing severe health problems.

Katie

Katie was a newly qualified schoolteacher. Most weeks during term time she worked fifty hours-plus. She said that she had always wanted to be a schoolteacher, and enjoyed the actual teaching side of the role. When she wasn't working she was always thinking about work. At first she was upset about the behaviour of some of the children but more recently she was concerned about getting her paperwork in order, or worrying that she did something wrong during a lesson. I often hear from schoolteachers that it is not the day-to-day issue of teaching that is the problem – although she did find some of the children's behaviour draining – it is, in Katie's words, the 'endless bureaucracy and accountability' that goes with it. She was constantly worried that she may have upset a child or said the wrong thing to a parent as her head was unsupportive and would more often than not back the parents.

Katie dreaded the morning staff meetings as the head had a habit of picking on one or two teachers. Her head was the type of manager who was not only quick to find fault, but also failed to praise people when they were doing a good job. Katie found it difficult to unwind and do anything constructive during the evenings; even when trying to relax by watching TV or reading a magazine, her mind would wander to school issues. She said the school was always at the back of her mind. 'Am I prepared for tomorrow?', 'Did I say the wrong thing last week?' Even when ill, Katie would force herself to go to work rather than face the wrath of her head for daring to be sick.

Katie used to be a good sleeper but her sleeping patterns had dramatically changed since she started at her new school. She told me that she had difficulty getting to sleep as her mind would keep turning over, thinking about the meeting the following morning. She also found herself waking up during the night and not being able to get back to sleep. Because of her work worries she found it very difficult to relax and to do anything constructive in her spare time that wasn't associated with work. She was constantly tired.

Katie looked forward to her weekends, especially Friday evenings and her lie-in on Saturday mornings. However, she didn't really do much at the weekends as most of her Saturdays were spent lying on the sofa, and Sundays were spent catching up with housework and domestic chores. Sunday evenings were 'ruined' (her word) as she began to think about work again the following day.

Even though Jessica and Katie work in completely different occupations, their life stories share many similarities. Both women are constantly tired, and have no time to pursue interests away from work. Interestingly, like a lot of people I speak to, they also enjoy what they do. Moreover, both of their lives are completely consumed by work: Jessica's, however, is consumed by the amount of work she does, while Katie's is consumed by constantly thinking about work and not being able to unwind post-work. Jessica is a good example of how we can easily get trapped by the demands of work and not be able to see a clear way out. Her main problem was that work took centre stage and she had unrealistic expectations of the demands she placed upon herself. Simply put, she didn't give herself enough time to relax and unwind. Katie's problems are a little more complicated as some of her stress comes from her boss, but her main issue was that she couldn't switch off after work to allow herself to unwind. Unfortunately, Jessica and Katie's experiences are not uncommon: many people have told me similar stories. Fortunately, as we shall see in the following chapters, both cases are relatively easily resolved.

The joy of work

Take a moment to think about why you work. If you ask most people why they work, the first, typical answer is for the money. We need to pay the bills, etc. Apart from the obvious need to earn money, consider other reasons why you work. Another way to ponder this question is to think about and focus on what you would miss if you didn't work.

Psychologists have discovered that people not only work to earn a living, to feed themselves, pay the mortgage and go on holidays, etc., but they work because work offers other rewards: it activates and stimulates, provides structure to our lives and allows for social contact with others, and gives us a reason to get out of bed in the morning.

Many workers dream of becoming rich, and many play the lottery as a short cut to richness. Researchers who have interviewed lottery winners have come to the conclusion that winning the lottery does not make us happy. Why is this? The majority of people who stop working following their win, say they miss work: the routine of getting out of bed, the sense of fulfilment and their work colleagues. Although it may not always appear so, work is actually good for us. The effects of work on health and wellbeing have been demonstrated in hundreds of studies. People in work report more happiness, fulfilment, say they are physically fitter and have more active social lives, than unemployed people. Have you ever wondered why corporate bosses or professional sports people, who have millions in the bank, continue working? It cannot be for the financial rewards. At the time of writing, and according to *Forbes*, 'The World's Billionaires' annual ranking of the world's wealthiest people, there are 1,645 billionaires in the world, and I would bet my house that the overwhelming majority still work or do some form of work. Most people are intrinsically motivated to learn new skills and develop. Surveys suggest that even if we became financially secure most of us would continue to work. One study in the USA found that 84 per cent of men and 77 per cent of women said they would carry on working even if they inherited enough money so they wouldn't have to work. Thus, the motivation to work is not only because of the financial rewards.

Achieving the right balance

We therefore get so much more from our jobs besides the pay we receive. Work enhances our self-esteem; it becomes part of our identity and gives us purpose in life. Many friendships and marriages are formed through work, and positive social interactions at work have even been associated with improved cardiovascular and immune functioning. Like most things in life, you can have too much of a good thing. In the long term working too many hours is not good for our health and wellbeing. We need balance in our lives. You will be familiar with the saying 'All work and no play makes Jack a dull boy'. This proverb has been traced back to the Egyptian sage Ptahhotep (a very wise man, I think, and someone with ideas ahead of his time), who was alleged to have written it in around 2400 BC. In 1825, in *Harry and Lucy Concluded*, the Irish novelist Maria Edgeworth added a second line to the proverb, 'All play and no work makes Jack a mere toy'. This saying is as relevant now as it was 2,000 years ago: is important to achieve a healthy balance between work and play.

We are at a period in history that our ancestors could only have dreamed of. We have washing machines, vacuum cleaners, microwave ovens and the like, all of which take the toil out of living, and we don't even have to get up to make a phone call or get off the sofa to change the TV channel. In Western societies, we are fortunate to have all these labour-saving devices at hand. In addition, the working week has changed, and people are contracted to work far fewer hours than our forefathers were. In theory we have a lot more time at our disposal. So what do we do with all this extra 'free' time? I am afraid that many of us who are lucky enough to be in employment, use our (unpaid) free time to work or do work-related tasks. One obvious reason for this is that we all feel less secure in our jobs today because of the unstable economic climate. Also, work has become more interdependent. We need other people to provide us with the information we require in order for us to do our work. Sometimes this means speaking to people outside the normal working day.

Another reason is technology. Mobile communication has increased tenfold over the last two decades. There are more than 130 million active SIM cards in Western Europe alone, and this number increases year on year. Mobile communication has countless benefits. It is great to be able to phone friends, family and work colleagues from just about anywhere in the world at any time. Mobile technology, however, is a double-edged sword. The disadvantage is that we can be contacted 24/7, and unless we switch the phone off — which most people don't — we face the risk of constantly being interrupted or bombarded with electronic information. Much of this we don't really need. Many people are constantly in touch with the office and we can receive information all day and night — and then we wonder why we can't escape from work and switch off. It is as if we are literally tethered to our mobile communication devices. A key principle of switching off is taking control, and you should feel empowered to turn off your mobile device/s out of work hours without feeling guilty. More on this later in the chapter on using technology.

Working long hours increases the risk of heart disease

Isn't it ironic, then, that people in work are all working longer and harder than ever before? If we are not actually working, as in producing anything or doing anything important, we are probably thinking about work: what we have to do, what we forgot to do, or what we did wrong. Society is becoming more educated about technology, but we seem to have lost our way somewhat. It is not healthy for a responsible society to expect people to work as hard as they do. There are limits to how much work we can physically and mentally do in any given day. A number of studies have shown long working hours to be associated with poor health. For example, a study in Japan[1] examined the working hours of men between thirty and sixty-nine years old who had been admitted to hospital with an acute myocardial infarction (heart attack). These men were compared against a group of healthy men, matched for age and occupational level, judged to be free of heart disease following a medical examination. The results revealed that men who worked more than eleven hours per day over the previous month were two and a half times more likely to have been admitted to hospital with a heart attack. Similar results were found when the researchers examined the increase in working hours over the previous month compared to their normal pattern of working. Again, those who had increased their working day by three hours or more were two and a half times more likely to have an acute myocardial infarction. The data was re-analysed adjusting for known risk factors (smoking, a sedentary lifestyle, etc.), but there was no overall change to the results. Longer working hours were associated with a significant increased risk of having a heart attack!

The famous Japanese work ethic

The Japanese have a tradition of working long hours, and it is not that uncommon for people to literally work themselves to death. Interestingly, the Japanese have a specific word, *karōshi*, which can be translated as 'death from overwork'. Many Japanese companies now recognise the harm to health caused by working too much, and some organisations in Japan now limit the number of hours of overtime their workers can do over the course of the year; many now urge workers to leave the office and go home on time. Some even use public address systems to announce to workers the importance of rest at a certain time during the evening. It is good to see that companies are starting to become proactive in this area. Unfortunately, since many people have busy workloads not all can take advantage of this modern approach to working, but this new approach to work/

life balance has stimulated or motivated a new kind of behaviour. Instead of people going home and relaxing with their families or spending time on leisure activities or enjoying hobbies, many Japanese workers simply take their work home with them and carry on working. Thus, many workers cannot or do not take advantage of the new spirit of work/life balance. The Japanese even have a word for this behaviour, *furoshiki*, which translates as 'cloaked overtime'.

The prodigious Isambard Kingdom Brunel, perhaps the greatest British engineer of all time, died at the early age of fifty-three, some say because he literally worked himself to death. He did, however, smoke up to forty cigars a day and slept as little as four hours per night! The point being that people lead busy lives, and there is pressure on us all to do more, be better and for greater return. Unfortunately we can get trapped in this cycle, leaving ourselves little or no time for reflection and contemplation. Sometimes it takes a life-changing event — for example, a health problem such as suffering a heart attack, or a loss as in a divorce — to force us to take stock, and re-evaluate our priorities. In the next chapter I will discuss why it is important for our health and wellbeing to switch off from work.

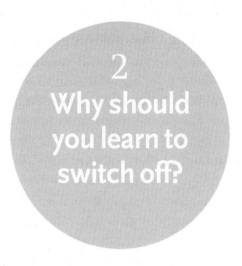

2
Why should you learn to switch off?

'A mind serene for contemplation'

John Gay

As we move away from a manufacturing economy to a knowledge and service economy, one of the biggest challenges facing workers today is learning how to de-stress and mentally unwind post-work. When I first started working in the area of stress, most research focused on the direct effects of the job on physical health. For example, we would measure workers' heart rates or blood pressure during work. Not too unsurprisingly, people who worked in highly demanding, stressful jobs showed higher heart rates and blood pressure at work compared to those who worked in low-demanding jobs. However, it gradually became apparent that stress levels at work was not the full story; rather, it was how people physiologically and psychologically unwind post-work that seemed to affect their health and wellbeing. Having increased blood pressure at work didn't matter too much so long as the person was able to unwind and reduce their blood pressure during their leisure time. I used blood pressure as an example, but the same applies for other physiological measures, such as cortisol and adrenaline. There is now a growing body of research evidence to suggest that the speed with which people 'recover' after a period of stress may have more bearing on the development of disease and illness than how reactive someone is during the period of stress. It appears that the effects of working in a stressful environment can — if we allow it to — 'spill over' into non-work time, and many people in demanding and creative jobs find it difficult to unwind after work and remain psychologically and physiologically aroused during their leisure time. With a rapidly changing environment, the economic instability and the complexity of the modern working world, it's time to develop a different way to think about work and leisure. Successful people have realised that they must learn to unwind and relax, and make time for themselves, and they appreciate that time spent away from work is just as important in terms of productivity and creativity than the hours they put in at work.

Nearly one in four people are annoyed because they cannot 'switch off' when not at work

Because you are reading this book I assume that you have recognised within yourself that you have difficulty psychologically switching off and unwinding from work. If so, you are not alone. For example, 'The Employment in Britain Survey' (1992) interviewed over 3,000 workers and revealed that 70 per cent of them found it difficult at times to unwind after work.[1] The survey also revealed that 72 per cent of individuals at some time worry about their job after work. Research also suggests that the proportion of workers who find it difficult to unwind after work and keep worrying about their job after work is increasing.[2] Our research has shown that approximately 20 per cent of individuals 'often' think about work-related issues during their leisure time and 10 per cent report that they think about work 'very often or always'. In addition, 24 per cent are annoyed because they cannot 'switch off' when not at work. There are approximately twenty-nine million people employed in the UK and this equates to 6.9 million people who, like you, find it difficult to unwind post-work. In the USA, there are approximately 120 million people in employment, in Europe approximately 220 million, so there are millions of people just like you.

People vary in the time it takes them to unwind post-work. Some people seem to be able to switch off as soon as they leave the office while others take considerably longer. It needs to be stressed, however, that it is OK to think about work at home so long as you do it in the right way (more about this in chapter 5). It is normal to think about work when you are not at work; we all do this to a degree. It only really becomes an issue when it starts to affect our health and wellbeing.

What do we mean by 'recovery'?

We need to give our minds time to rest and 'recover' from the demands of work. When psychologists talk about recovery in the work context, they generally mean something that has been lost and the process of returning to a former state. Work is often demanding, and in order to work effectively we have to expend energy during the day. We can think about the different forms of energy: cognitive (thinking/planning concentration, etc.); emotional (trying not to lose your temper when things go wrong or colleagues/customers annoy us); physical (doing manual work, or typing, or just sitting in the same position for most of the day if office-based); and physiological (the need to eat and drink). Thus, working requires effort expenditure, and draws on our physical, cognitive and emotional resources. When resources are stretched, due to high demands or stress, we begin to feel strained and in need of a break. Without sufficient recovery breaks, this can lead to fatigue and in the long term can develop into a number of other negative health issues.

Thinking about work in the wrong way can make you ill

As stated in chapter 1, it is widely accepted that working too many hours is physically bad for us. However, we know now that inadequate psychological recovery, or poor disengagement from work, is associated with a range of health problems including cardiovascular disease, fatigue, negative mood and sleep disturbance. For example, a prospective study — that followed up people over a period of three to four years — found that men who reported an inability to mentally relax after work had an approximately threefold increased risk of heart disease.[3] Another study showed that a lack of recovery over the weekend was the key contributor of the higher incidence of cardiovascular death among the employees.[4]

Each one of us will have different ways of handling the stressors of life, including the demands associated with work. Some argue that this ability is part of our genetic make-up, while others claim that we learn by experience. I am convinced it is a little of both. One thing that is clear, however, is that each of us is different in how much stress/demands we can handle, and all of us need to be aware of our stress threshold and to know when to stop and rest.

Recovering from work as an active process

To reduce the risk of developing strain symptoms, and to protect health long term, it is important for employees to recover from work demands. As discussed earlier, the term 'recovery' in the work context generally means something that has been lost and the process of returning to a former state in readiness to face further demands. In order for recovery to occur we need not only to physically distance ourselves from our place of work, we also need to distance ourselves mentally, and not to think about work too much when not actually working. I use the term recovery to describe the general process of recovering from work demands; however, the terms rest, relaxation, recuperation, recreation, restoration, respite, rewind, unwind, as well as recovery itself, have all been used to describe the process of disengaging and relaxing from work. However, for the most part the term recovery will be used in this book.

When we think of the term relaxation, we mainly mean relaxing our muscles after a period of energy expenditure; however, our minds also need to relax. We think of recovery as an active process, and it is not simply the case that in order not to think about work one needs to do nothing. If you are physically tired from working hard, it is good to relax by not doing anything too physical. However, if you are mentally tired or fatigued, sitting down to relax, e.g. watching television, is probably the least effective way to unwind. In such cases, doing something physical, as in going for a walk, gardening, swimming or housework, is the preferable option. It is interesting that the word recreation literally means to recreate, as in 'making again'. In order for you to recreate, you need to create time for recreation.

Take control and get more done

If you are intent on taking control of your life and experiencing a more balanced approach to your work, you have (no irony intended) to work at it. You can't expect instant results although you will, however, find some exercises in this book that will help you to distract yourself instantly from work. You will have to make lifestyle changes. The way to use this book is to approach each exercise with an open, inquiring mind. Give all chapters a go, and practise each exercise. I stress the word *practise*: you need to practise and rehearse each exercise. By learning to switch off and unwind, you will find that you feel more in control of your life. You will also find that you have more energy, are less fatigued, and generally more happy and healthy than before. You will also discover that you enjoy or find some exercises more useful than others, and this is to be expected. I have my own favourite strategies for unwinding and I will use them again and again. However, you will also realise that some strategies work better in particular situations and some in others. There is no one-size-fits-all. Feel free to modify the exercises to tailor them to your needs but please follow the basic formulae as presented initially: they have been proven to work.

We all need physical time away from work, and we also need mental time away from work. We all need to take time away from our work-related thoughts in order to take control and re-energise ourselves. Due to the fuzzy boundary between work and home, we need to change the way we think about our leisure time. It is no longer practical or even feasible to consider work as the active part of our day and our non-work time as passive leisure. We need to start thinking actively about how to 'switch off' from work in order to enjoy our free time, to protect our health, have more energy and sleep better. By doing this, we will also find that we get more done the next day. The aim of the following chapters in this book is to help you in this process.

I have based this book on material I have presented and delivered in a series of workshops and research papers on stress and recovery from work. Over the years I have found that some exercises work better than others and I have only included those that have been successful. I have arranged the exercises in this book in no particular order; you may find some exercises work better than others, or you may prefer certain ones more than others.

3
Are you overworked?

'In a disordered mind, as in a disordered body,
soundness of health is impossible'

Cicero

Look at the table opposite. It contains a number of negative health symptoms. Read each one and place a tick next to the ones you experience. Don't think about your response too much, just read them and tick the box that applies. Be honest with yourself.

Do you experience any of the following: concentration problems, fatigue, irritability, restlessness, poor sleep? If you do, it's not surprising as all these symptoms have been associated with people failing to adequately 'switch off' and unwind from work. Every ten years or so, the Office for National Statistics on behalf of the Department of Health, the Scottish Executive and the National Assembly for Wales conducts a survey in the UK to assess, among other things, adult mental health. The survey is quite comprehensive and contains questions about health, wellbeing, work, stress and a host of demographic and social factors. In 2010, the government made public the data of their 2007 survey. This survey interviewed 7,461 adults living in the UK, and of those approximately 5,000 people said they were in full-time employment at the time of the interviews.

Anxiety	☐
Concentration	☐
Depression	☐
Fatigue	☐
Irritability	☐
Problems getting to sleep	☐
Staying asleep	☐
Waking up too early	☐
Worry	☐

In addition to the questions reported above, the researchers also assessed the difficulty people had in switching off from work, for example, 'When I get home, I can easily relax and switch off from work'; 'Work rarely lets me go, it is still on my mind when I go to bed'. Using the data from this survey Professor Fred Zijlstra from Maastricht University in the Netherlands and I were able to identify two groups of individuals. One group consisted of people who find it incredibly difficult to mentally disengage and switch off from work; we call this group high ruminators, and compared these with workers who reported they find it easy to mentally switch off and unwind post-work; we call this group low ruminators. The word rumination comes from ruminant and refers to the way cows and other such mammals chew over regurgitated food. Because they eat grass and grass is not easily broken down in their stomachs they have to chew it constantly. When we psychologically ruminate, we chew over the same thought or image in our heads. For example, we could ruminate about giving a presentation, chairing an important meeting, an important looming deadline, or dealing with other potential stressors at work. The thought seems to go round and round even if we try not to think about it. When we ruminate we typically do so in order to make sense of or find a solution to a problem, to stop feeling bad, or, ironically, to try to stop ourselves from ruminating! You may ask, but what is the difference between ruminating about work and just thinking things through to try to improve something? The short answer — more on this in chapter 5 — is that ruminating involves emotional thinking: people who ruminate about work become tense and annoyed because they can't stop thinking about work.

Going back to the study, what we found once we adjusted the data for age and gender was that high ruminators were approximately 4.3 times more likely to report fatigue, 4.5 times more likely to report irritability and 3.5 times more likely to report sleep problems, relative to the low ruminators. Thus, people who find it extremely difficult to stop thinking about work during their leisure time experienced many more negative health symptoms relative to those who could stop thinking about work. In addition, compared to low ruminators, high ruminators — those workers who found it difficult to switch off post-work — were a staggering 6.5 times more likely to report concentration problems. Although it is not possible to say conclusively that failure to unwind and free oneself from work-related thoughts caused people to experience these symptoms, the evidence nonetheless looks pretty convincing.

Cows are not the only ruminants

Rumination is pervasive and ruminative thoughts are typically goal-driven. When we ruminate, we do so in order to look for a solution to a problem or to try to comprehend the meaning of a stressful situation. Our goal is to stop feeling stressed and in order to do this we naturally try to find reasons for being stressed. Often the thing we ruminate about is emotionally driven. Why did that person say that to me? Why does my partner not want to see me any more? In the work context, our boss may have ignored us in the corridor and we assume this was due to something we have done wrong: 'Is it because she does not like my work?' This makes us feel anxious, sad or annoyed, and then we search for reasons why. The problem with emotionally driven rumination is either that often there is no correct answer or it is not possible to find the answer because there is no issue in the first place. That, or it only existed in our heads. However, when we ruminate we try to generate a number of alternatives, but we soon tend to challenge and dismiss the explanations we generate. We find no solution that is perfect and this leads us back into the cycle of rumination. I will discuss the role of rumination in more detail in later chapters, and in the next chapter you will be able to see for yourself what type of work-related ruminator you are.

We now know that the effects of work demands/stressors may be long felt both physically and psychologically, even when the object causing the strain response is no longer present. For instance, a person who has a quarrel with a colleague at work may continue to think and ruminate about the encounter post-work during their leisure time, or a person who has made an error may ruminate about the possible consequences if the error is not corrected. In doing so, they may experience the same physiological level of arousal that originally accompanied the stressor.

Someone who can't switch off from work and ruminates about, say, a quarrel at work, may show elevated blood pressure and heart rate even a week after the argument when they reflect on the experience. This suggests that the reactions to stress can be sustained over a long period of time, particularly in individuals who repeatedly think and ruminate about the stressor; and persistent failure to unwind following a period of stress arousal wears down the body's physiological restorative system. Unwinding following a stressful working day is therefore necessary in order to prevent further wear on the physical organism and aid reparative function during the night.

I once interviewed a teacher who told me that Fridays are the worst days. Teaching is generally recognised to be a stressful occupation, and this teacher said that if anything bad happened on a Friday (e.g. he had a problem with a particular child or parent), he would ruminate about it all weekend. He would have to live with the issue and play it over and over in his mind even though he knew there was nothing much he could do to rectify the situation until the following Monday.

Constantly thinking about work and not adequately unwinding wears down our bodies' natural resistance and can lead over the long term to a reduced immune response. One sign of a weakened immune system is a reduction in our ability to fight off common colds and infections. You may have noticed that stressed people at work are those who are off sick or come to work with a cold. In our studies, we also find that people who ruminate, and who find it difficult to mentally unwind post-work, are also those who report a higher frequency of common cold symptoms, e.g. sore throats, coughing, sneezing, stomach upsets, etc.

Our studies suggest that it may not necessarily be work demands per se that cause negative health problems, but the failure to unwind from work properly that is the critical factor in this process. It is therefore important that you develop an understanding of your own unwinding process and learn how to unwind adequately and switch off from work during your non-paid working hours.

Relaxing the body

The exact mechanism underlying the association between unwinding, or lack of unwinding, and health is not clear and is still hotly debated. However, there is very good evidence to suggest two distinct pathways are involved: the physiological and the behavioural.

Our biological system has evolved over millions of years and is a very efficient system for dealing with stress in the form of threats, and our bodies are particularly good at dealing with acute stress. We have an innate response known as 'fight or flight'. First described by Walter Cannon in 1915, the fight or flight response basically suggests that when animals perceive threat from a potential predator they have two choices: they either fight − if the attacker looks weak or smaller than they are − or, if not, they run like mad! (There is actually a third alternative: some animals play dead.)

Although not fully understood, two involuntary branches of the autonomic nervous system are thought to be closely linked in the progression from stress to disease: the sympathetic nervous system and the parasympathetic nervous system. When the body is under threat or stressed, sympathetic activity (or parasympathetic withdrawal) mobilises the body for action by initiating physiological arousal, such as increasing blood pressure, heart rate, catecholamine and corticosteroid secretion. In the absence of threat or perceived stress, the parasympathetic system counteracts the effects of sympathetic activity and restores homeostasis. These two mechanisms serve to protect the organism in the short term, but can have damaging effects if stress is prolonged.

For many of our everyday threats neither flight nor openly fighting (even if we believe we are right and our boss is a complete jerk) is wise, as we are likely to get more than a bloody nose. In most organisations, as in the natural world, there is a hierarchy, and people are expected to bow to those in authority. There is a hierarchy even when people are sharing similar positions or levels as they jostle for rank within or between organisations. This can take the form of trivial point scoring, such as showing no interest in what is being said, or being unresponsive and distant. Disregarding colleagues is really a form of intimidation; more seriously, if it is not stopped, it becomes a form of bullying. On one level this may be considered normal, a result of the natural order of the world — the survival of the fittest. More likely, however, this happens when the aggressor has a deep sense of inferiority or jealousy. People may also be stressed about having too much work to do, about having unfinished tasks at work to complete, or about a problem at work such as trying to learn a new computer system; or perhaps it is just down to an individual at work. The result is the same — people will feel threatened. In a strange way, people can also stress themselves. Not getting your work done can be a threat to your ego or self-esteem. Some people who don't need to work continually will nonetheless keep working and will not know when to stop. Therefore, we need to learn to cope with the perceived threat in another way.

When we face threat in the form of a stressor the body responds by releasing a hormone called cortisol. Many people perceive cortisol as an important biomarker for stress, and this is partly true. However, what cortisol secretion actually does is to prepare the body for action. Up to a point a greater cortisol release indicates that a person can deal effectively with the stressor/transgressor. When an individual is faced with a stressful event the hypothalamus-pituitary-adrenal axis (HPA) responds by activating corticotrophin releasing factor (CRF) and adrenocorticotropic hormone (ACTH) neurons in the paraventricular nucleus (PVN). This causes the adrenal cortex to release the stress hormone cortisol. If people are consistently exposed to high stress, this may result in a suppressed immune system in the long term.

The HPA axis response will vary depending on the perceived causes of stress; for example, if the situation is uncontrollable or unpredictable a greater degree of activation may occur. Chronic cortisol reactivity has been associated with a number of negative health indices, including cardiovascular disease risk factors, cognitive functioning, depression, colds and infections. We do not know exactly how and why cortisol works, but it is clear that it is a very important hormone that plays a major role in a multitude of health-related problems and is essential to proper body functioning.

Cortisol secretion exhibits a stable diurnal pattern, peaking within the first thirty to forty-five minutes on awakening, and then declining over the day, reaching its lowest around 10 p.m. Cortisol is inversely related to melatonin, the hormone that is associated with sleep. When cortisol levels are high, melatonin will be low. Likewise, when cortisol is low, melatonin will be high. The initial sharp rise in cortisol on awakening, known as the cortisol awakening response (CAR), is a distinct feature of the diurnal pattern of cortisol secretion, and is considered a marker or indicator of the integrity of the HPA axis.

In one of our studies we sampled a group of 108 schoolteachers[1] (teaching being recognised as a stressful profession) and asked them to provide us with a sample of their saliva at 10 p.m., and then an additional four samples: one on awakening and then fifteen, thirty and forty-five minutes after waking up. Our underlying aim has always been to provide useful feedback to each teacher so they can learn how to reduce their stress levels and how to unwind from work themselves. Before giving us their saliva samples, the teachers also reported how much they were thinking about work over the previous hour (for the evening reading) or how much they were thinking about work once they woke up in the morning. We then divided the sample into high ruminators (those teachers who habitually find it difficult to unwind and switch off from work) and low ruminators (those who habitually find it relatively easy to unwind and switch off from work). Cortisol secretion was found to be significantly greater in the high compared to the low ruminators at 10 p.m., and this effect was not related to leisure activities or work patterns during the evening. For the morning measures, high ruminators demonstrated a flattened CAR relative to the low ruminators and this effect appeared to be associated with sleep disturbance during the night due, in part, to work-related thinking. Thus, it appeared that ruminating about work-related issues was associated with cortisol secretion.

Relaxing the mind

Another way unwinding or lack of unwinding affects health is via our behaviour. The behavioural pathway between unwinding and health can be influenced by many factors. Leading a sedentary lifestyle, drinking alcohol to excess, smoking and moderating eating habits have all been implicated in the aetiology of disease, and all may be involved in the process of unwinding and health. For example, individuals who smoke or drink alcohol, and who find it difficult to unwind from work, may increase their smoking and/or alcohol intake as they feel this will help them relieve the psychological consequences of stress, such as tension or anxiety. Too much alcohol consumption, lack of exercise and smoking have all been linked with negative health and a reduced lifespan. However, the good news is that there are also behaviours that can help the unwinding process and increase longevity, health and wellbeing. Thus, workers can choose to unwind by using behaviours associated with positive health, for example, socialising, meditating, exercising and playing sport. These and similar activities will be discussed in further chapters.

As reported in chapter 2, there is some evidence to suggest that failing to mentally unwind after work is associated with an increased risk of cardiovascular disease. To reiterate, the prospective study reported in chapter 2 found that men who reported an inability to relax after work had an approximately threefold increased risk of ischaemic heart disease, a disease characterised by reduced blood supply to the heart. The coronary arteries supply blood to the heart muscle and a blockage in the coronary arteries reduces the supply of blood to the heart muscle. One well-known mechanism that can result in an increased risk of ischaemic heart disease is atherosclerosis. Atherosclerosis is a serious disease and occurs when arteries become clogged by fatty substances, such as cholesterol. If people eat diets rich in saturated fats, this can increase the fatty build-up in their arteries. Over time this can lead to a complete blockage similar to the way limescale deposits eventually cause water pipes to block.

To investigate possible mechanisms between failing to unwind post-work and heart disease risk we asked people to complete a questionnaire about how they habitually think and unwind from work and also to complete a log of their snack food intake.[2] We divided people into high and low groups depending on whether they could or could not easily mentally switch off post-work. We also divided the foods into healthy (e.g. fruit, vegetables) and unhealthy types (e.g. biscuits, crisps, chocolate, cakes). When we looked at people who thought about work issues in a detached, non-emotional way — what I call problem-solving ponderers — we found no difference in the consumption of either type of snack foods between those high and low in this construct. We also found no difference in terms of the types of snack that high and low detachers nibble on during the evening. What we did find, however, was that high affective ruminators — those who become tense, annoyed and upset because they can't stop thinking about work issues post-work — ate more unhealthy types of foods (more cakes, crisps, chocolate and biscuits) compared to people who did not think about work in this emotional way. This suggests that people are using food in order to regulate their emotions, in other words to make them feel happier. Unfortunately, in doing so they are also putting their health at risk because they are consuming more saturated fats in their diet. Another interesting finding from this study was that people who told us they could easily switch off from work were also those who prepared a cooked meal most evenings. It appears that having to cook and prepare a meal diverted attention away from their work-related thoughts. High ruminators, those who found it more difficult to switch off, reported a higher frequency of eating processed foods (meals that require little or no mental effort to prepare) than low ruminators. Simply putting a carton in the oven or microwave requires little thought and is unlikely to divert attention away from work.

These results suggested that failure to unwind from work is not necessarily related to unhealthy food choices as individuals who thought about work in a non-emotional detached way did not appear to eat a higher percentage of unhealthy snack foods relative to those who did not think about work. The crucial factor appears to be the type of thinking that people engage in post-work. Moreover, this study highlighted the harm that thinking about work can cause if done in an emotionally negative way.

It is clear that failure to unwind from work and constantly getting stressed by thinking about work issues is damaging to our mental and physical health. The next chapter discusses how your failing to adequately unwind from work can also damage your company's health.

4

Why your boss should be interested in unwinding

'A healthy workforce is an efficient and productive one'

Mark Cropley

I t has long been established that employers have a legal duty of care to their employees. Employers must provide a safe working environment and the necessary equipment for doing the required task. It is also reasonable, I think, to expect employees not to be so tired at the end of a working day that they have no energy or time for social, recreational or educational activities during their off-work time. Given the increased intensity of work and the demands of modern living in the 24/7 economy, fatigue is a common, almost universal, aspect of life. Fatigue has been called a modern epidemic. Research suggests that between 11 and 30 per cent of workers in

Europe are seriously affected by work-related fatigue and in the USA abnormally high fatigue levels have been identified among 14.3 per cent of men and 20.4 per cent of women.

Fatigue is the modern epidemic

The term fatigue is used in many different areas and currently there is no single accepted definition that meets the criteria. However, fatigue needs to be distinguished from sleepiness. Sleepiness is the tendency to fall asleep; fatigue is the body's response to sleep loss or to prolonged physical or mental exertion. Fatigue may be *reduced* by sedentary activity or rest without sleeping, whereas subjective sleepiness and the propensity for sleep are often *exacerbated* by sedentary activity or rest. For example, we often feel sleepy or sluggish on a Sunday, particularly if we have not been active. Researchers have also attempted to distinguish between acute and chronic fatigue but it is difficult to know exactly when acute fatigue becomes chronic. Acute fatigue, however, is short-lived and we all normally experience this at the end of a working day as the body's way of telling us that we need to rest. Chronic fatigue builds up over time if we do not listen to what our body is telling us and continue to push ourselves with little rest. There have been many tragic accidents in which fatigue has played a crucial role.

Employees need to have sufficient time to recover from work demands, and replenish lost resources in order to prevent the build-up of fatigue. As stated earlier, recovery generally implies gaining or retaining something that has been lost. Working in a demanding job leads to an increase in strain reaction such as tiredness and fatigue. In order to reduce and reverse such strain reactions, individuals need to spend time away from work, and in particular refrain from work-related activities during their leisure time. It is important for employees to recover from work, particularly when the work is demanding or especially stressful. Not unsurprisingly, studies have shown that employees who feel refreshed before they return to work also report they are more engaged at work, and feel they are performing at a higher level.

A tired worker can be an unethical worker

When I started to investigate the process of unwinding from work, I had a hunch that people who can't or who don't unwind from work during their leisure time would display negative health symptoms. This, as we have discussed in the previous chapter, was relatively easy to demonstrate. What I didn't know at that time, and what came as a surprise, was that failing to unwind and poor recovery from work is also associated with a number of other behaviours that can affect not only productivity but also how people behave at work.

In a series of interesting laboratory and field studies, Christopher Barnes at the Pamplin College of Business, Virginia Tech, has revealed that lack of sleep leads to high levels of unethical behaviour at work. Put simply, ethical behaviour can be considered as behaviour that is legal and morally acceptable to the wider community, whereas unethical behaviour is either illegal or morally unacceptable. An example of unethical behaviour at work could be false reporting of accounts, inappropriate sexual conduct or theft. In one study, for example, 182 full-time employees and their supervisors agreed to participate in an online study. Each worker was asked to complete an online survey including measures about their job demands, fatigue and sleep, over the previous three months. The supervisors completed their responses three weeks later, and rated the frequency of ethical behaviour of the employee over the previous three months. Examples of unethical behaviour in this study varied, from 'claiming credit for someone else's work', 'divulging confidential information', 'doing personal business on company time' and 'concealing one's errors' to 'passing blame for errors to an innocent co-worker'. The supervisor rated the frequency of ethical/unethical behaviour on a 7-point scale, from 1 = never, to 7 = frequently. The results showed a clear and significant correlation between poor sleep and the supervisor's rated unethical behaviour. Moreover, the association between poor sleep and the supervisor's rating of unethical behaviour was mediated by fatigue, meaning that poor sleep led to feelings of fatigue that were associated with unethical conduct at work.

In a not too dissimilar type of study, Michael Christian (University of North Carolina at Chapel Hill) and Aleksander Ellis (University of Arizona) investigated the association between sleep deprivation and workplace deviance in nurses from a major medical centre in the south-western United States. Workplace deviance was assessed with statements such as 'discussed confidential information with an unauthorised person', 'used an illegal drug or consumed alcohol on the job', 'worked on a personal matter instead of working for your employer' or 'said something hurtful to someone at work'. Again, the results showed that sleep deprivation increased workplace deviance. Moreover, they found that those who slept six hours or less were statistically more likely to engage in deviant work-related behaviour compared to those who slept more than six hours per night. Thus, this and other research findings support the notion that recovery from work and good sleep are crucial for health, productivity and morality in the workplace.

Barnes argues that the reason why fatigued individuals engage in such practices is due to what another psychologist, Professor Roy Baumeister, calls ego depletion. Baumeister believes that self-control requires sustained effort maintained by cognitive resources that are themselves depleted by the act of engaging in self-control. Self-control requires exerted effort, and as people have only a limited capacity

– rather like having a limited fuel supply – sustained self-control takes its toll. When this occurs an individual is less able to suppress or resist the temptations that they would normally manage to do with a full tank and as such that individual is more susceptible to engaging in otherwise unethical practices. According to Baumeister, sleep is essential for replenishing the depleted cognitive resources, as posited in the ego depletion model.

A rested worker is an engaged worker

Another area of work in which poor recovery affects performance is what is called work engagement. Work engagement is a state of being cognitively, emotionally and behaviourally connected to one's work. Organisations reap clear benefits when their employees are fully engaged in work. Engaged workers will persist with tasks and are highly dedicated; they have more energy and enthusiasm for tasks compared to less engaged workers, and they tend to become immersed in their work. No wonder companies spend vast sums of money on hiring consultants to motivate their staff to become more engaged. A cheaper option might be to encourage staff to adopt good recovery/ sleep practices such as going to bed at a regular time, and not working too late in the evening, as research has shown that worker engagement can be influenced by poor recovery behaviour. In a study of 328 responders who completed an online questionnaire survey, individuals were asked to complete measures of sleep and sleep practices (called sleep hygiene), together with a measure of work engagement. The engagement measure assessed three different ways or factors by which people connect to their work: absorption, e.g. 'I was immersed in my work'; vigour, e.g. 'At my work, I felt bursting with energy'; and dedication, e.g. 'I was enthusiastic about my job'. Responders give a rating on a 7-point scale ranging from 0 (never) to 6 (every day), and ratings are averaged to create one work engagement score. The results showed that those respondents who frequently engaged in poor sleep hygiene behaviour were also less engaged in their work.

Continually thinking about work can affect work engagement in a number of ways. However, there are two most obvious mechanisms. Firstly, rumination directly affects sleep. As stated in the previous chapter, rumination is the term psychologists use to describe the process whereby an unwanted thought goes round and round in our heads. When individuals ruminate about work they find it difficult to fall asleep, they report more disturbed sleep and they feel unrefreshed when they get out of bed in the morning. In the short term, this leads to acute fatigue, and people find they can't work as effectively the following day. This is normally a temporary problem, remedied by a good night's sleep. Over time, however, if sleep is continually disturbed this can lead to chronic fatigue. In order to preserve their remaining depleted energy levels, people naturally become less engaged and put less effort into their work. Secondly, thinking and ruminating about work, the tasks you have to do, the meetings you have to attend, deadlines that are nearing or co-worker issues, etc., uses up valuable energy reserves. If we do this too much without a break, our energy reserves become depleted. Ruminating takes up a lot of our energy resources. When our reserves become depleted naturally we are more likely to be less engaged and less focused at work, and, incidentally, more likely to make mistakes.

Do you sometimes forget what you went upstairs for?

Do you have difficulty remembering people's names, do you sometimes forget appointments, or go into a room at home for something and then forget why you went there in the first place? Have you ever tried to open your house with your car keys? These are what psychologists call cognitive failures. Everyone makes a cognitive failure occasionally but we find that people who find it difficult to unwind from work, and ruminate about work issues, make more cognitive failures on average. In fact, we have found a clear linear association between how frequently one ruminates about work and the number of cognitive failures one makes. We find this particularly true for those people we call 'affective ruminators', those who become tense, annoyed and frustrated because they cannot switch off from work-related thoughts (more about this in chapter 5). Often cognitive failures can be quite annoying but also amusing; but sometimes a cognitive failure can have tragic and devastating results, as in the Piper Alpha explosion in July 1988 and the capsizing of the *Herald of Free Enterprise*, just outside Zeebrugge harbour, Belgium, in March 1987. Incidentally, human error accounts for approximately 90 per cent of all road accidents. I am not saying that these accidents are caused by rumination, but our chances of making a cognitive failure increase if we find it difficult to switch off from work. Even if lives are not at stake, it can be embarrassing or even costly if you accidentally press the send button before an email is completed or forward an email without properly checking the content first. I am not suggesting all cognitive failures can be avoided, but clearly if people are adequately rested or have had time to psychologically detach from work, the chances of making such errors are substantially reduced.

Switch off and be a good colleague

Being adequately recovered from work can also pay dividends for organisations in other ways. Some behaviours within organisations may be intangible and not be part of a job description but nevertheless when performed well can bring many benefits to an organisation.

One such behaviour that has been identified is what is called Organisational Citizenship Behaviour. Organisational Citizenship Behaviour has been defined as an:

> *individual behavior that is discretionary, not directly or explicitly recognized by the formal reward system, and that in the aggregate promotes the effective functioning of the organization.*[1]

Typically, an employee would not be trained in such skills, as Organisational Citizenship Behaviour tends to be the result of personal choice by individuals who have certain personality characteristics. Such individuals 'go the extra mile' and go beyond the call of duty. People who perform this role in organisations do not normally get rewarded for their endeavours, and, indeed, Organisational Citizenship Behaviour is difficult to monitor and measure in any accountable way. However, such unselfish behaviour has countless benefits that can permeate the organisation.

In a series of studies, a German research professor, Carmen Binnewies, and colleagues show how important gaining sufficient recovery can be for fostering Organisational Citizenship Behaviour in the workplace. In one of her studies, 358 employees working with individuals with special needs completed two sets of questionnaires six months apart. Following the analysis of the results, Professor Binnewies found that feeling recovered during leisure time predicted an increase in task performance after six months. In addition, positively reflecting about work was found to predict an increase in proactive behaviour (personal initiative, creativity) and Organisational Citizenship Behaviour. Such results emphasise the role of positive non-work experiences for employees' job performance. In another study, Professor Binnewies showed that when employers felt sufficiently recovered after the weekend, they also demonstrated higher levels of performance at work, more proactive behaviour and more Organisational Citizenship Behaviour.

Being successful and productive at work *does not begin and end there*. Success is a process that *starts* at home. Being able to unwind, relax and recuperate during non-work time will build up resilience. While most would agree that some stress is expected within the workplace — as we all need to be challenged from time to time — this should be kept to the minimum. Many issues of stress relate to fatigue and exhaustion, and are due to worry and not being able to sleep. Lack of sleep leads to total exhaustion. Psychologically detaching from work during leisure time refers to the process of switching off. Being too fixated on work, and continually thinking about work issues during one's leisure time, drains energy and leads to impaired wellbeing, increased cognitive failures, less engagement and an increased risk of deviant behaviour at work. Psychologically detaching from work facilitates the recovery process and helps to restore energy levels. Thus, workers who are sufficiently recovered from work are more focused at work, more productive and are healthier and more collegial when they are at work. Therefore, a healthy balance between work and leisure is clearly a win-win situation for both employees and their organisations. Employers should educate, encourage and develop strategies to help employees psychologically detach from work. A detached and well-rested worker will be more engaged at work, happier and more productive than one who is overcommitted, anxious and unrested.

When it comes to unwinding and switching off from work, our work has shown that we are not all the same and that there are clear differences in the way we all unwind. Some people can easily mentally detach from work, while others find it extremely difficult and get frustrated and annoyed because they can't stop thinking about work issues. The first step is to identify and clarify how you think about work during your free time. The next chapter presents the work-related rumination questionnaire. By using the questionnaire you can see what type of post-work thinker you are.

5

Test your own
off switch

'People's personalities can get in the way
of their own work'

Mos Def

It is not uncommon for people to think about work and work-related issues during their leisure time. This is only natural. We spend the majority of our day working or performing work-related tasks. More than a third of our day is spent working or getting to or from work, and we probably spend more time interacting with people at work than we do with our partners and friends. It is not surprising, then, that we think about work a good deal. We all act and think in different ways, and we all act and think about work-related issues in different ways.

People often ask me if they should try to avoid thinking about work issues completely when not at work. This is a good question, and over recent years the concept of work/life balance has attracted much research and media interest. One school of thought suggests you should keep the two worlds apart; however, I don't think this is really possible or desirable unless you find yourself working in a really mundane job. Also, I think the term 'work/life balance' is a poor one: it implies that we can never reach complete harmony in life as we are constantly struggling and spending our energies trying to keep these two worlds both level and balanced. Therefore, according to this view we are all living in a slightly precarious position, trying not to let one world dominate the other. So, when people ask if they should try to avoid thinking about work during their leisure, the answer really depends on the type of thinking they do about work, and whether their work-related thoughts affect their health and wellbeing. If thoughts are intrusive, and you would rather not be having them, then you need to detach completely from work as much as you can during your free time. If you use your free time to think about the positive aspects of work, you socialise with work colleagues, you find that you are more creative when not actually at work, or you find solutions to work-related tasks/problems, then thinking about work when not actually being paid for it is not a big issue. It only becomes an issue if it affects our health and wellbeing. Everyone, however, should have time away from work. When we can't switch off and have a lot on at work, we may become moody and tense, or we may have difficulty sleeping or staying focused. In the short term this is not really a major issue: it is just part of the vicissitudes of life. There are times when we have tight deadlines and we have to push that little bit harder, but this is not a major concern if we know we have planned some quality downtime afterwards.

How do you unwind post-work?

In order to see what type of person you are in terms of your post-work thinking, complete the Work-related Thoughts Questionnaire in the table below. When completing the measure, respond in terms of how you typically think post-work.

Work-related Thoughts Questionnaire

The following questions relate to your time after work. Please circle the number that applies to you. Read each question carefully but don't spend too long thinking about your answer as your initial response is normally the most revealing.

		Very seldom/ Never	Seldom	Sometimes	Often	Very often/ Always
1	I become tense when I think about work-related issues in my free time	1	2	3	4	5
2	After work I think of how I can improve my work-related performance	1	2	3	4	5
3	I feel unable to switch off from work	1	2	3	4	5
4	I am troubled by work-related issues when not at work	1	2	3	4	5
5	I get fatigued by thinking about work-related issues during my free time	1	2	3	4	5

		Very seldom/ Never	Seldom	Sometimes	Often	Very often/ Always
6	I leave work issues behind when I leave work	1	2	3	4	5
7	I make myself switch off from work as soon as I leave	1	2	3	4	5
8	I tend to find solutions to work-related problems in my free time	1	2	3	4	5
9	I become irritated by thinking about work issues when not at work	1	2	3	4	5
10	In my free time I find myself re-evaluating something I have done at work	1	2	3	4	5
11	I find thinking about work during my free time helps me to be creative	1	2	3	4	5
12	I get annoyed by thinking about work-related issues when not at work	1	2	3	4	5
13	I think about tasks that need to be done at work the next day	1	2	3	4	5
14	I am able to stop thinking about work-related issues in my free time	1	2	3	4	5
15	I find it easy to unwind after work	1	2	3	4	5

Check your score using the key below. For example, to see whether you find it easy to detach from work add questions 3*, 6, 7, 14, 15 to give a total score. We have identified three types of ways individuals think about work-related matters when not at work: Affective ruminators, Problem-solving ponderers and Detachers. For each type, your score should range from 5 to 25. I will explain what each means below.

	Affective ruminators	Problem-solving ponderers	Detachers
Questions	1, 2, 3*, 4, 5	6, 7, 8, 9, 10,	11, 12, 13, 14, 15
Total			

* = (reverse scored)

By completing the questionnaire you will be able to see what type of post-work ruminator you are, and you will also be able to compare your own profile against the wider working population. We have used this questionnaire in a number of studies and workshops and you can check your scores by shading in the quadrant below.

Which category do you fall into?

	Affective ruminators	Problem-solving ponderers	Detachers
Low (5–10)			
Median (11–19)			
High (20–25)			

Do you recognise yourself? This is not an absolute measure. You will probably find that you are high or low in a couple of factors. Now what does it mean to be a high problem-ponderer or a low detacher?

The wrong way to think about work after work

Affective ruminating

Affective ruminators are people who in their free time find it difficult to escape emotionally from their work-related thoughts and become tense and frustrated because they cannot stop thinking about work issues. Affective rumination is a cognitive state characterised by the appearance of intrusive, pervasive, recurrent thoughts about work, which are negative in emotional terms. If left unchecked, thinking about work-related issues will become cognitively and emotionally intrusive during leisure time. Following a demanding or stress-provoking experience at work you may have tried actively to avoid thinking about work-related matters during your free time, but it is likely that by doing this you may even have thought about work more, or work issues popped into your head when you least expected them to, while watching TV, or speaking to your spouse/partner, for example. Such thinking is associated with negative emotional reactions which can manifest themselves in the form of tension and annoyance. When you feel this way your mind keeps churning over the same issue. This clearly has a negative effect on unwinding or your restoration from work.

Not unsurprisingly, this type of thinking is associated with a number of health problems including anxiety, feeling low (or depressed), concentration problems, fatigue and difficulty with sleeping. Most people with this characteristic also report problems getting to sleep and if they wake up during the night tend to start thinking about work-related issues. People will often say that they feel tired but as soon as their head hits the pillow they just lie there and start thinking about work issues; that is, the things they need to do at work. Their mind keeps going over the same issues, and they toss and turn for ages until they eventually fall asleep. Most high-affective ruminators report disturbed sleep and feel unrefreshed in the mornings. I have included a sleep questionnaire in chapter 27, where I discuss a range of techniques you can use to improve your sleep. We have found, too, that workers who score high on affective rumination also experience more common colds and ailments compared to those scoring low on it.

High 'affective' ruminators find it extremely difficult to switch off and constantly think about work, or work-related issues, when not at work. They may find themselves working late, and checking emails, and when they socialise their conversation inevitably revolves around work. Below are responses from two people we interviewed who scored high in affective rumination. Such responses are quite typical:

> *'If it's really bad it can intrude on everything. It can intrude on your social life, it can intrude on your sleep; it can intrude on your relaxation.'*

> *'If I haven't got as far as I want, then that [her work issue] will bug me and it will sit there in the back of my mind and frustrate me until I can get it sorted ... I take work home with me mentally ... but not in respect of actually to be able to do anything with it.'*

The right way to think about work after work

Problem-solving pondering

The second state we call 'Problem-solving pondering'. Problem-solving ponderers are people who think and ponder about work-related issues when not at work because they enjoy their work and the challenges work gives them. They like the mental challenge of solving a problem and may choose to think about work-related issues when not at work because they find the process interesting ('I find solutions to work-related problems in my free time'). This form of thinking may be characterised by prolonged mental scrutiny of a particular problem or an evaluation of previous work in order to see how it can be improved. For an organisation perspective it may be extremely beneficial for employees to think about work during their free time, as this may lead to effective problem-solving, for example, the development of new plans, strategies or ideas, or the creation of new products.

Even when problem-solving ponderers are not actively engaged in problem-solving, a solution to a problem they have been pondering may suddenly pop into their head. Many of us have probably had a similar experience when we were doing the gardening, for example, or watching a film and not really thinking about work: suddenly an idea will appear from nowhere. Sometimes this may be triggered by an apparently unrelated comment or something you are reading.

Problem-solving ponderers enjoy thinking and learning new skills and have an innate willingness to actively engage in learning and developing themselves. For them, work — when they are working in the right environment — can be more of a hobby, so much so that the days just pass by. This happens when we enjoy our jobs. For problem-solving ponderers thinking is an end in itself. This is called autotelic thinking. Autotelic is a thing or process described as 'having a purpose in and not apart from itself', and has its roots from the Greek *autotelēs*, from *aut-* + *telos*, meaning self + goal. An autotelic writer likes to write; an autotelic musician loves to play; the autotelic artist loves to paint. To become expert in these fields individuals need to practise and craft their skills over many years, but they do not see this as a chore.

Thus, individuals who engage in problem-solving pondering enjoy the challenges and particularly the act of solving a problem. These people tend not to be stressed or annoyed by thinking about work outside work. Indeed, this unemotionally detached form of thinking can be quite therapeutic and beneficial. It is interesting that we can come up with our best ideas or the best ways to solve problems when we are not in the office or not even consciously thinking about the problem; sometimes the solutions just pop into our heads. Although people high in problem-solving pondering find it highly enjoyable and stimulating to think about work issues when not at work, these types of people still need to schedule — and they do — some downtime in order to reflect, and to prevent fatigue in the long term. However, confirmed problem-solving ponderers tend to report a high level of control and autonomy in their lives. Thus, they enjoy work but also find time to have fun. They are typically psychologically and physically healthy.

Some people have no difficulty switching off ... because they never switch on

Detachers

The third type of people we identify are called 'detachers'. Detachers are those who tend to switch off as soon as (or relatively quickly after) they leave work. Being a detacher does not mean people cannot lead a productive and rewarding working life. On the contrary, people are more effective at work if they feel rested and refreshed after a good night's sleep. Thinking about work, especially late at night, delays sleep onset and then interrupts sleep once you have dropped off. It is all about balance. If people are too detached from work, this suggests to me that they were never really engaged in the first place. A job has to be stimulating and rewarding intellectually as well as financially. If you never think about your work or your colleagues outside work, it suggests to me that you are in the wrong job. It is, once again, all about finding a good work/life balance.

For instance, Kelly said,

'I would say I'm pretty good at switching off and after I leave the office and ... getting home, I do tend to leave work at work ... I'm

just one of those people that as soon as I've stepped out of the door, I just switch off.'

The aim of the rest of the book is to introduce you to techniques and exercises you can use in order to make you less emotionally attached to your job outside of work. My goal is not to make you completely forget about work issues during your leisure time; as I have already said, I don't think this is wise or realistic. It is important that you read the whole book but I suggest you practise the techniques in each chapter and in this way gradually work through the book. It is best not to try to do everything at once, as you will not be able to keep this up and you will feel that the techniques are not working. Therefore try to master one or two strategies before you try the next. In addition, you will find some techniques work better for you than others. This does not mean that they do not work at all; they simply don't work for you. We are all different; certain techniques suit some people more than others. All I suggest is that you keep an open mind. Also, be kind to yourself. Don't worry if you do occasionally think about work. I will show you here how to let such thoughts pass. Unwinding is an action-oriented process, and by this we mean that an individual needs to develop and apply self-initiated activities in order to recover from work. Stopping ruminating and learning to unwind from work is an active process. It is also a dynamic process that changes over time. Therefore I do urge you to practise as much as you can. Unfortunately, I cannot point you to an off switch in the brain, but I can assure you of success if you follow my advice.

Once you have read and mastered the various techniques, return to this chapter and complete the detachment questionnaire again (see page 52). You will be surprised at your progress. You may also see that you have become more productive at work, are happier and enjoy life more.

Developing
your switch-off

Overview

The first part of the book discussed why it is important for you and your boss not to be dominated by work. My goal was to convince you that in order to be productive and successful you don't have to work extensive hours and wear yourself into the ground. You can still get as much or even more done by taking your foot off the gas pedal now and again. I also introduced the notion of work-related rumination and why it is important for health and wellbeing to relax the mind and switch off from work during your free time. There are various techniques and strategies you can adopt to help you do this and in Part II, I present exercises and strategies you can follow to develop your own off switch. All the exercises are relatively easy but will require you to take time out to practise. However, in order to change you first need to be mentally prepared and motivated to change, and in the first two chapters in this part I discuss why and how you can change your approach and core beliefs about work and the way you think about work. I also include a small section about overcoming perfectionistic tendencies. Again, I emphasise that by changing your approach to work, this will in no way compromise your productivity. Indeed, ironically, by changing your core beliefs about work you will find that you can get more done.

6
Your core beliefs about work

'It is not the strongest of the species that survive, it is the one that adapts successfully to change'

Charles Darwin

It may be difficult for people to stop working especially if they have developed a habit of working excessively long hours over a number of years. Years of unrelenting work can develop in us a 'core belief' that we must work all the time, e.g. 'If I don't work this evening I'll become a failure', 'If I don't work my boss will think I'm lazy', or 'I must work or I will never be successful'. As a society we applaud those with what is called a 'strong Protestant or Puritan work ethic', and in many respects this is an admirable quality. It is very good psychologically for people to engage in and enjoy their work, and be productive. It is also good for society in general. However, some people not only work excessively, they become obsessed with work. For them work and leisure seem like two opposing forces, and leisure becomes devalued and loses out. Such people have little time for family, hobbies or time to engage with community activities outside of work. The notion of a healthy work/life balance for these people simply does not exist; their philosophy of life is 'life is for working'.

At the extreme end of the work and leisure continuum are the so-called 'workaholics', the people who seem to be completely obsessed by work, and their work/leisure balance is completely out of line. In fact, there is a clear negative relationship between work and leisure: the more they work the less they spend time on or are interested in life outside of work, including their interest in family activities and friends.

Take, for example, the case of Joe, a sales manager with a team of fifteen people who is clearly a workaholic. Joe took part in one of our studies, and during the interview in response to the question 'How do you prioritise your work and home life?' he said:

> *'Workwise, I just see work. I have people to manage, so it's making them more efficient for getting things done. Just make sure I know when all the deadlines are so I know when I can make it. My home life, we just do what we feel like at the time. There is no real prioritising.'*

Another question put to Joe was 'if you have a demand at home (that will take some of your time away from work), or a demand at work, what would be your priority? How would you handle that?

> *'I think work would win out, unless it's very important at home, I would have to do it. You just have to deal with the situation. You know if we are going through a due diligence, then that normally wins. Even when dealing with home matters I would be thinking about the issues I need to deal with at work. It is not good to be out of the office too much.'*

Although Joe is an extreme case, there are many people who are verging on workaholism or have workaholic tendencies. Indeed, many people I commonly encounter have a habit of working long hours, and they don't see it as an issue before it is too late. Even if people are not physically at work, their minds will be on work issues. Take the case of Bill. Bill worked in finance, and described how he regularly works *'upwards of fifty-five or sixty hours a week'*, but, rather than see this as a lack of personal choice, his perception was that *'long hours go with the territory'*. He added,

> *'Whether I work at home, work on the train, I don't think about it as being overtime, it's just part of the job. I think my standard hours are between thirty-five and forty hours a week.'*

This behaviour is fine in the short term but working excessive hours is not good for long-term health and wellbeing or conducive for a social or family life. By the way, one of Bill's complaints was that he couldn't unwind and switch off from work. This was obviously due to the fact that he was always working.

The average American spends more than five hours a day watching television

When workaholics or people with workaholic tendencies are not working (I have deliberately avoided the word 'relaxing') they tend to spend their time on what we call escapism activities. These are passive leisure activities such as watching television because they are too tired to engage in creative or active hobbies, etc. In fact, people with 'workaholism tendencies' spend most of their non-working time watching television. It is interesting that watching television is the number one leisure activity in the Western world. It is estimated that the average European watches approximately 3.43 hours of television a day, and the average American spends 5.11 hours per day watching television. A staggering 32 per cent of Britons watch three hours or more television per day, the second highest in Europe to Bulgarians, while only 13 per cent of Germans watch three hours or more television on a daily basis. Spending too much time on passive activities will eventually lead to health issues. Gaming is also another escapism activity which is for the most part sedentary. Spending long periods of time on such activities can be as bad for health as smoking and obesity.

Workaholics actually dread leisure and are obsessed about using their time productively, or what they think is productive. No wonder they don't enjoy leisure: they never learnt how to play. The few who do play tend to treat their leisure as they would their work: they strive to be the best at what they are doing. If they play squash, golf, or run, they play with a competitive, must-win approach. OK, most of us like to be competitive, but what sets us apart from the workaholic is that we enjoy the game. The enjoyment comes from the participation and winning, if we are lucky enough to win, is a bonus.

The tendency to work excessively is governed by an inner core belief that productivity in whatever form (producing more goods, being more creative, creating more sales, better quality, etc.) equates to being a better person. In fact, the behaviour of a workaholic is counterproductive and eventually they burn out. It is not possible to continually push, and then push some more, without adequate rest and recovery; and doing so will have long-term health consequences. As a group, workaholics are more likely than the average person to experience stress and fatigue, and are more likely to suffer from physical (but mostly preventable) ailments, such as high blood pressure, ulcers and headaches. A body fuelled by adrenaline and caffeine is bound to burn out sooner or later. It is also not surprising that many workaholics are in unsuccessful relationships as they have neither the time nor the emotional need for their partners or children.

Be engaged but not obsessed

The smart and productive workers are those we call 'engaged workers'. Engaged workers have high energy levels and strongly identify with work, but they do not display 'workaholism tendencies'. Thus, engaged workers are connected to their work but they demonstrate a positive attitude to it. They have high psychological wellbeing and are very proactive in their jobs. There are many characteristics of the engaged worker. They have bags of energy, dynamism and drive. They take pride in their work and the company they work for. An engaged worker becomes absorbed and fully enmeshed in their work and are more likely to go the extra mile when called to meet deadlines. Typically, the engaged worker also tends to be loyal to their employer and will remain in the same company for many years; a clear benefit for the organisation. A worker who is fully engaged is clearly an asset to any company they choose to work for or are very successful if they work for themselves.

You can never be successful if you leave work on time

You may not have heard of Sheryl Sandberg, but I am certain you have heard of Facebook. At the time of writing Ms Sandberg is the Chief Operating Officer of Facebook. She has been described as a 'tough and fearless woman', and clearly she is very bright and dedicated to her work. Her advice to young professional women (and men) is 'Work hard, stick with what you like, and don't let go'. Prior to joining Facebook in 2008, she worked at Google, the World Bank and the US Treasury Department. Sheryl is in charge of business operations at Facebook, including sales, marketing, business development, human resources, public policy and communication. Clearly she is a busy person. Interestingly, she is famous for leaving her office at 5.30. She does this in order to have dinner with her family and spend time with her children. She stated:

'I did that when I was at Google, I did that here, and I would say it's not until the last year, two years that I'm brave enough to talk about it publicly. Now I certainly wouldn't lie, but I wasn't running around giving speeches on it.'

At first Sheryl would feel she was being negatively judged for leaving work 'on time', and she used to compensate for this by sending emails late in the evening or early in the morning, in order for her co-workers to see that she was not slacking. Only recently has she felt comfortable leaving the office at 5.30. It is a shame that in today's 'presenteeism' culture there is a stigma associated with going home 'on time'. I deliberately wrote 'on time' as I don't mean leaving early or slacking off. This is very apparent in highly competitive work environments when you are not really a team player if you don't stay until the cleaners have left. There should be no guilt attached to leaving work on time. Admittedly there may be days when the whole team will have to work late or even pull an all-nighter, but this should clearly be the exception, and certainly not the rule.

Research has also shown that eating with your family has many benefits. Children tend to do better at school, are happier and healthier, and less likely to get into trouble if they eat dinner with their siblings and parents. Conversely, an employee works more efficiently and is more engaged if he or she has a happy home life. We need to get the message across that it is OK to leave work on time. In fact, why don't we make this mandatory?

Is it possible to change?

Interestingly, studies that have examined the relationship between workaholism and engagement find there is no correlation. That is, the two constructs are mutually different, and are independent psychological states. Indeed, research tells us that it is also possible to decrease workaholism tendencies while at the same time remaining or becoming more engaged in one's job. In order to change your working habit you need to change your core belief about work. You will not truly be able to unwind and relax during your leisure time until you sincerely believe that it is good to do so. This will happen over time as you gradually find yourself being more productive at work, less fatigued and more enthusiastic about work, but this may take a while. Changing one's core belief will take time. While you are in the process of changing your core beliefs about work you will inevitably experience tension between your new inner dialogue and your long-standing belief that you have to work sixty-plus hours a week. There will be many nights and weekends at first when you will feel anxious when you are not actually working or thinking about issues at work. You may experience the 'should I check those emails just in case?' syndrome ... but it is important you try to fight these types of urges.

Learn to accept change

Core beliefs are the glue that holds us together and gives us a purpose in life. Core beliefs are very important as they also help us to deal and cope with the stressors. In the late seventies, Suzanne Kobasa was working as a consultant psychologist for the Illinois Bell Telephone (IBT) company in Chicago. Back then, the telephone industry in the USA was a federally regulated monopoly, which meant in effect that most people at the company had a job for life. In 1975 Suzanne Kobasa started to collect data on a group of approximately 259 volunteers on stress and strains, personality characteristics, social interaction patterns, motivation and beliefs. In addition, along with the psychological data, her team also collected data on aspects of job performance.

Working in this type of industry was very different in the seventies. Most workers felt secure and had a job for life. This was soon to change as the federal government started to legislate for more competition between businesses. Six years into the programme there was upheaval in the whole sector due to more competition under new free market conditions. The IBT workforce shrank from roughly 26,000 in 1981 to just over 14,000 in 1982. Those lucky enough still to be employed found their roles repeatedly being reorganised. During this period and for the following six years, Kobasa's team continued to collect performance data. What became clear quite early on in the research was that many employees, approximately two-thirds of the group, became psychologically distressed by the changes. Symptoms included the classic signs of psychopathology – anxiety, depression, more suicides, divorces and addictive behaviours. Physically, those who became distressed by the changes were also more likely to suffer from heart attack, stroke, kidney failure and cancer. However, this wasn't the case for the final third. This group showed few signs of these symptoms, and in many ways seemed to be thriving. As a group, they showed more excitement, enthusiasm, motivation and fulfilment than before the upheaval. These people were less affected by change and were clearly more resilient. Kobasa termed this behaviour hardiness. Hardiness is a pattern of attitudes and strategies that can be grouped around three Cs: challenge, commitment and control. Challenge: hardy people accept that life is by nature stressful, but they see stressful situations and challenges as opportunities to grow. Commitment is the belief in the importance of staying involved with the project or task, and not giving up or stopping trying. Control implies the need to try to stay focused and in charge of the situation; people who feel in control focus on what they can control or influence, and not on tasks or situations outside their control.

Further research has suggested that hardy people (those high in hardiness traits) have what are called anchors in their lives. When we are committed to something, anchors give us purpose and create meaning in our lives. Hardy people who are committed to a purpose and have certain core beliefs tend to be more motivated and find time to reflect on their values and beliefs. Such anchors remind them of what they are doing and where they should be going. Hardy people are social people; they take an interest in friends and work colleagues, and are engaged in what they do.

7
Changing your core beliefs about work

'Believe you can and you're halfway there'

Theodore Roosevelt

The previous chapter introduced the notion of core beliefs about work and the willingness to change. This chapter contains an exercise that will help you recognise and change your maladaptive core beliefs about work. I have also included a section on the core belief of perfectionism and offer advice on how to reduce 'perfectionistic tendencies' if you have them. By following the exercises you should nonetheless achieve your goals, become more engaged and therefore get more done at work.

Core beliefs refer to the type of beliefs people have about work and how committed they are to their organisation. The first exercise, on page 75, is aimed at helping you change your core belief about work and life. It is important to point out that by doing the exercise you will not become less engaged and less committed to your job. In fact, I am advocating the complete opposite. Many people have a strong work ethic but are still able to relax and unwind. These people are just as or even more productive than overcommitted individuals. This exercise is therefore designed specifically for people who have a strong Protestant work ethic, who are very committed, but find they are never able to switch off and unwind properly. If you are one of these people you need to stop this way of thinking before it stops you — permanently. The aim of the exercise is actually for you to rethink your approach to work and the core belief you hold about work. By doing this, you will find you get more done, as you will be more focused and less fatigued at work. In order to achieve our goal, there are certain steps we need to go through.

Rethinking work

First, we need to identify your present primary core belief about work and examine its validity. You can use Core Belief Worksheet I on the next page. Write down examples/evidence relating to or supporting your present core belief (column A). You will have a number of examples that all relate to one core philosophy. It is surprising that people don't realise how much work dominates their life until they have actually written down examples and seen them on paper. Writing something down makes it seem more real, and by writing down your core belief this exercise will increase the likelihood of you consolidating your new healthy approach to work. For example, you may find that you check your emails every evening, even just before you go to bed. You then write down the reason why you are following that behaviour.

Core Belief Worksheet I: Your present core belief (old self)

A Collect evidence of the behaviours that support your (present) core belief about work	B Collect evidence for the motives/reasons behind your behaviour	C Collect evidence to oppose that behaviour
(*example*) Checking emails all evening (even when out with friends)	(*example*) I need to check emails or I will fall behind People like it when I respond to them quickly It makes me feel important ...	(*example*) I will not fall behind as I won't take on too much work Most people will not expect an instant response outside of work I know it is better for me to concentrate on what my friends are saying and enjoy the night out and it is rude to check emails in social situations
(*example*) I need to work until 9 p.m. every day		
(*example*) I worked through lunch		

Next you need to explore the evidence that supports and contradicts your present core belief. It may be you believe your boss will think more of you if he can contact you outside work. You may feel that you can get more work done if you work longer hours (actually the evidence suggests that you just slow down and work less efficiently once you pass the fifty hours a week mark). You may think 'there is no one else to do the work if I don't do it', or 'people rely on me to respond to them quickly even outside of work'. Write the reasons for your behaviour in column A in column B. There are a number of reasons as to why we do certain behaviours and you need to be honest with yourself if you really want to change. For example, you may check emails to impress upon your friends that you are important, or you may feel you need to impress your partner that you are busy and successful.

Next, generate reasons or evidence that contradict or oppose this behaviour/belief in column C. You need systematically to evaluate the data that supports or contradicts it. For example, you may ask people what they think or ask your friends if they think the behaviour is rational. Recognise the failings in your behaviour that support your old (present) core belief as this helps you to reconstruct realistic ways of changing that belief and behaviour.

Core Belief Worksheet II: Your present core belief (new self)

On this sheet you write down behaviours you put in place to help you change your old core belief into the new you (column C). You then systematically evaluate the data that supports or contradicts it (column D). Recognising the failings in your old core belief will help you to start to reconstruct a more realistic view of life.

C What behaviour have you decided on to help you change your core belief?	D Collect evidence of behaviour that supports or contradicts your new core belief
(*example*) Not to check my emails after 7 p.m.	(*example*) Last week when out with friends, even though I was tempted, I didn't once check my phone for messages or emails
(*example*) To stop working during my leisure hours and spend time with my family	...
(*example*) Pursue my hobby	...

Even when you are in the process of change, note down and collect evidence to support the old belief. For example, when you found yourself working in the evening or when you found yourself checking emails when you were socialising. Be honest with yourself if you had to work or check emails because of a specific deadline; don't feel guilty, as this will sometimes happen. Just note it down and let the thought pass this time but try not to repeat this behaviour.

You need to do some homework, preferably on a weekly basis. Collect evidence that supports your new philosophy towards work and life. Remember that top workers have a positive attitude to both work and life; they counterbalance the demands of work by pursuing healthy leisure activities and enjoy spending time with family and friends. They actively invest in leisure activities. So take time each week to review your progress. Many of my clients have told me that writing down and recording their progress helps them to stay focused on the task. They also say that by using this method they can identify previous bad behaviour. What surprised some people is the frequency with which they do work-related tasks outside work. If you have a partner you could ask them to help you here. Often they may be more truthful about you than you are about yourself. Writing down and recording your behaviour will help you to consolidate your new core belief and increase the likelihood of your taking control of your life.

You can use this worksheet to tackle other problems, too. Now and then you may need to review some behaviours and beliefs over time, and the information you put into the worksheet. Over time, too, you should find that you develop a more realistic set of beliefs. Sometimes in life we can never find the answer until we write the problem down. When I have done this in my workshops people often say that once they have written something down it suddenly became so obvious that they needed to change their approach to work. They find themselves wondering why they didn't do it before.

Start slowly

It is sometimes difficult to adopt your new core belief and you need to plan and practise. Start slowly; think of it in the same terms as you would if you were trying to get fit. You wouldn't run a marathon if you have spent most of your life on the sofa, so don't expect to be able to stop working immediately. Fitness takes time, as does developing a healthy approach to work. You need to change your habits gradually. One of the reasons why people put on weight and stop dieting is because they find it too difficult and reduce their food intake too much, too quickly; therefore they always feel hungry and crave food. Don't be afraid to start slowly and don't be put off. (See the case study below.)

Remember the case study of Jessica in chapter 1? Jessica had, or was approaching, workaholic tendencies. She worked sixty-plus hours a week, was always fatigued and complained she could never escape from work. Ironically, someone looking from the outside could quite easily think Jessica had the perfect approach to work. On one level her work conditions were what a lot of people strive for. Her job meant that she was free and flexible, could choose her clients and was relatively well paid. However, Jessica's worst enemy was herself; she was putting more and more pressure on herself by taking on too much work and then worrying about whether or not she could cope. She was constantly ruminating about work when she wasn't working. One of the first things we did when we met was to go over Jessica's core beliefs about work. I wanted to know what drove Jessica. Was money the driving force? Was the fear of failure? Or was something else driving her? It turned out that one of her chief worries was having no work at all. The thought of being out of work was really upsetting, especially as she had been made redundant from her last job even though she put her heart and soul into the company. She was worried that if she started turning work down eventually it would dry up. We worked on this issue.

As reported in chapter 1, Jessica had a few difficult clients who took up a great deal of her time. There is the 80/20 rule of thumb that says 80 per cent of the rewards come from 20 per cent of the work. This is based on the work of an Italian engineer, Vilfredo Pareto, who observed the distribution of wealth in society and concluded that roughly 80 per cent of wealth and income was generated by roughly 20 per cent of the population. Although this is not exact science it is a good rule of thumb, and so Jessica and I worked together on identifying her most profitable and least profitable clients as well the most difficult and least difficult ones. We reasoned that so long as Jessica could make a decent living there was nothing wrong with working with good clients/colleagues even though they didn't always pay top dollar. There may be other rewards; for example, they might be easy to work with, they might introduce you to other clients, and they might just be nice people you don't mind spending time with. We decided, on balance, that it was better for Jessica to drop her most difficult clients, the ones that took up 80 per cent of her time but who certainly did not give her 80 per cent of her returns. We also worked on a couple of other issues that I shall cover in this book, such as filling the void, developing a hobby and planning mini breaks (discussed in chapters 11, 12 and 17) in order for her to have something to look forward to, and for rest and recuperation.

When I met Jessica four months later she felt a lot more in control, and in her free time was going to the gym and developing new hobbies. Obvious, perhaps, but sometimes it takes someone else to point out the obvious. Maybe it was me telling her to dump (recommend they find another financial adviser) the time-wasting, difficult clients, as it legitimised Jessica's own belief. Did it reflect badly on her? Of course not; she was actually very good at her job, and, besides, she had a portfolio of very good clients who valued her work. In the long term her other clients would gain and, by being more relaxed, refreshed and committed, Jessica became more engaged and stopped making mistakes.

When I next saw Jessica she was a different person. She felt more in control and was having a life outside work. She also was glad to see the back of her time-wasting clients.

It is often said that people can't live with change unless they are ready for change, and changing one's core belief is no different. The motivation for change needs to come from within. The key to change is finding what you really want out of life. Ask yourself if you are ready to change; if you decide you are, you have a very good chance of succeeding.

Is perfectionism holding you back?

Do you always strive to be the best? Do you aim to make your projects 100 per cent perfect? Do you check everything over and over again, and is nothing ever perfect in your eyes? Furthermore, do you also find that more often than not you are late with a project, or you just get it in on time? If some of this rings true, you are probably a perfectionist.

There are many advantages to being a perfectionist; if you are, such traits have probably served you well over the years. You may convince yourself that you wouldn't have got to where you are now if you had a sloppy approach to life. True, there are many advantages to being a perfectionist: you are probably very good at planning, well organised and controlled, and you are good at foreseeing potential problems and building contingency plans.

There are also, however, many disadvantages to being a perfectionist. You may set yourself unrealistic targets, and expect similar very high standards from others. Perfectionism can serve you well but if you are given extra work or have deadlines to make you may find your stress levels build up. Because you focus on the smaller details, you sometimes don't see the bigger picture, such as getting the project finished on time. Perfectionists sometimes make poor managers because they expect very (sometimes impossibly) high standards from their subordinates, and they may stop delegating work because it is never good enough. Therefore, not only do they alienate their work colleagues, they also end up giving themselves too much work and too much stress.

Some people divide 'perfectionistic' tendencies into two types: adaptive and maladaptive. Adaptive perfectionism is characterised by high levels of conscientiousness, high personal standards, high levels of organisation and a desire to achieve personal goals. By contrast, maladaptive perfectionism is characterised by an intense fear of failure, a high need to present and protect a 'flawless image' and ego. Maladaptive perfectionism has been linked with the high need for self-concealment. People high in this personality trait have a need to conceal mistakes and imperfections. This is probably due to their irrational belief that if something is not perfect it is a bad reflection on themselves. It is therefore important to establish in your mind that you as a person didn't fail, but your behaviour did. You can change your behaviour with practice.

Due to the self-concealment nature associated with maladaptive perfectionism, people high in this trait often withhold sensitive and potentially embarrassing information from others and they rarely seek out or utilise existing social support networks. In comparing adaptive versus maladaptive perfectionism, the former are less likely to ruminate about their stressors, are less likely to become depressed and are less self-critical. Thus, although adaptive perfectionists set themselves extraordinarily high standards they do possess the flexibility to allow for occasional mistakes and they ultimately derive a real sense of satisfaction from their successes.

Perfectionism has been associated with extreme difficulty unwinding and switching off post-work, and it's not surprising as perfectionists simply don't know when enough is enough. They are constantly looking for 'perfection'. We often talk about the law of diminishing returns; hours of effort may only produce a very slight improvement in the task you are working on. This is often formulated as 'the gain is not worth the pain'. It is not surprising that high perfectionism is associated with a number of stress-related physical and psychological disorders, including anxiety, depression, fatigue, coronary heart disease, eating disorders and obsessive compulsive disorder, to name a few.

Don't be too critical about yourself

Let's accept that there is no such a thing as perfection. If there were we would simply stop moving forward; there would be no point in doing so. We have to accept that. It is good to strive to be better at something, but not to beat yourself up if things don't always go to plan. Looking back with disdain over a piece of work you have done is not a rational way of approaching life. It is good to learn from experience but don't remain in the past. You can't move forward with the next chapter of your life if you continually reread the previous chapter. We need both imperfection and failure in order to move forward. Science is full of failures. Think for the moment about the invention of the humble light bulb or the bagless vacuum cleaner. All the ultimate, successful inventions were the result of past failures — or thinking from a different perspective. If we didn't experience failures we would never know what it was like to be successful. I think it was Thomas Edison who said that he never failed; he just found 10,000 ways that didn't work.

There are a number of reasons why we put off tasks, and sometimes it is simply that we don't like doing them. We can always find something more interesting to do. However, for the perfectionist, procrastination is not as straightforward. A perfectionist may delay getting things started as they can't find the best way — in their minds — to approach the project. They may put off sending important emails as they worry they may have made a mistake or that the email does not quite convey what it is meant to. It seems quite irrational but many of us do this. Many high-level perfectionists live in a state of high tension, they are full of self-doubt, have high anxiety and always want to be seen in the best light in order to support their fragile self-esteem. This is why they ruminate and worry so much about their work, and why it is important that we change our perfectionist ways if we really want to unwind from work. Therefore, take action, and don't be too critical of yourself.

Write it down

Flashcards

Flashcards are notes to yourself. They are used to reinforce what you have learnt, and to remind you to adhere to your new core belief. These can be used when the going gets tough, but you should also have some cards made simply to remind you of the key points from this book, that you look at on a regular basis. You can also list the behaviours you need to adopt in a given situation. For example, in fighting the urge to work through your lunch break. When you have the thought about working through lunch, you may try convincing yourself that it is only for today. However, check with the card on which you have written: 'It is very important to take lunch. I need to relax, and I will be more productive, make better decisions and be less tired in the afternoon if I do.' Traditionally these words were written on a piece of paper or an index card, but nowadays as most people have smartphones it is easier to write your statements directly into your phone. But some people may find the cards better, as it seems more personal when you see your own handwriting.

You can also use some cues to help you. First you write down what your initial thought might be, and what feelings you associate with that thought. Next you generate a counter-thought (what can you do to persuade yourself against the initial thought?), and then you make an action plan. For example, it's been a busy day, you have difficulty stopping work during the evening and your adrenaline is still pumping:

Example 1

If you find yourself working late when you know it's really not necessary:	
Initial thought:	If I carry on working there will be less to do the next day.
Feeling:	I feel disappointed and workshy if I don't carry on.
Counter-thought:	I have done a lot already today and a break will do me good. If I stop now I will feel more refreshed in the morning and more engaged at work tomorrow.
Action:	I need to distract myself from the urge to work and take some time to unwind in order to be more productive tomorrow.

Example 2

Thinking you need to work all the time in order to be successful:	
Initial thought:	If I stop working now I will never be successful.
Feeling:	I am a failure if I go home at 5.30.
Counter-thought:	Sheryl Sandberg goes home every day at 5.30 and she is definitely not a failure.
Action:	I will stop now and spend some time doing what I want to do.

Example 3

If you find yourself becoming distressed by thinking about work one evening:	
Initial thought:	I am useless, my mind is racing and racing, I have so much to do.
Feeling:	I have no control over my work-related thoughts.
Counter-thought:	I can distract myself as I have done it before.
Action:	I am not going to sit here. I am going to do something constructive (e.g. this might be going to the gym/work, spending time on a hobby, or sharing time with family/friends).

Example 4

Knowing when to stop because of your perfectionist traits:	
Initial thought:	This work is really not good enough to show my boss and I must take it home to do some more on it.
Feeling:	I would be embarrassed to submit this work and I am useless.
Counter-thought:	I'm being pathetic, my boss is normally pleased with my work and even if it is not 100 per cent it would be good to get some feedback from him.
Action:	I will stop now and give it to Jack.

The purpose of the flashcards is to give you support when you are feeling vulnerable and to reinforce what you have learnt and know. You can use flashcards as a tool to remind yourself of your previous successes, you can develop your own to be used in conjunction with any chapters from this book, and by using them you will feel more in control of your life.

8

When thinking about work issues spirals

'The mind is its own place, and in itself can make a heaven of hell, a hell of heaven'

John Milton, *Paradise Lost*

Sometimes we become so preoccupied with a situation at work that we lose perspective and total sense of control and the majority of our thought processes become directed to the situation at work: 'I can't believe he/she said this', 'Why is my boss always nasty to me?', 'How could I have been so foolish?', 'This is my only chance to make a good impression', 'If only I hadn't said that to Jenny, I wouldn't be in the mess I am in now'. If left unchecked these issues can dominate our leisure time, and consume all our emotional and physical energy. The problem with this kind of thinking is that for the most part we feel there is nothing that can be done, especially when we have these thoughts outside of work.

One schoolteacher I spoke to told me about a situation in which he had been involved. He had an unblemished career and was a very good teacher. We will call him John for now. One day John saw one of the children messing about in an electrical cupboard. Why he was in there was another issue. However, noticing the danger in this boy's actions, John grabbed him and yanked him out of the room and out of danger. End of story, or so you would have hoped. The following day the boy's parents came into school and accused John of physical assault, claiming he had manhandled their son. Instead of praising John for saving their son's life — or preventing serious harm to him — they were trying to sue the school and ultimately end the career of this well-respected teacher. This incident took place on a Thursday and wasn't resolved, so John had all weekend to dwell on and ruminate over the issue. He became trapped in a vicious circle of continually thinking that this one incident could lead to him losing his job after nineteen years of teaching, even though his action was justified. In the end, common sense prevailed and it was all sorted out, but John had a couple of sleepless nights.

How thinking about work worries can spiral out of control

As stated earlier, we use the term rumination in psychology to describe our thought processes when we become trapped and begin to focus on the same issue, and the issue plays over and over in our heads. We repeatedly think about and become preoccupied with something in particular and we are unable to get it out of our minds; for some people this is like a CD being stuck on the same track and being played over and over again. In the same way, those who ruminate may replay the same argument over and over in their heads. They become more upset and emotional and because they become emotional they ruminate more, thus conjuring up a vicious circle of negative thinking. People who ruminate about work issues become preoccupied with work and work-related issues, and can't stop thinking about work. We also know that people who are prone to ruminate about work issues are more likely to report stress and experience fatigue.

In part, rumination is a normal process. Thinking about an issue can be helpful especially if it leads to our coming up with a good solution. If we did something wrong, or said something out of place at work, and we have suffered for our actions, then a short spell of rumination makes it less likely that we will repeat the mistake. Only when ruminative thinking becomes excessive, and we can't escape from such thoughts, does it become problematic.

Ruminative thoughts about work issues can be triggered by what I call a hidden trigger mechanism, a term borrowed from Nikola Tesla, the great Serbian-American inventor and engineer. A hidden trigger mechanism is something that, once unleashed – and under ideal conditions – can generate a vast amount of energy and cause utter destruction and devastation. Tesla observed that a small snowball, once released down a mountain, can grow and grow until it eventually gets so large and heavy that it creates an avalanche and starts to take out vegetation, rocks, trees and anything else that stands in its way. Similarly, an apparently innocuous thought, or something said in normal conversation, or even a seemingly unrelated object, can trigger a work-related issue that we would rather not be thinking about. Such thoughts can be triggered spontaneously and they can occur when we least expect them. We might be watching television and suddenly something in a programme will remind us of some (negative) event at work. If not checked immediately, once started the thought gains momentum and goes over and over in our heads, spiralling out of control. Long-term rumination can develop into anxiety and depression, and when this occurs some people will need to seek professional help. Over time, the thought eventually loses its emotional content and melts away (as with snow) but the damage may already have been done. This is why it is good to tackle issues early on before they snowball out of control.

The anticipation is the worst thing!

It is good to try to anticipate problems and take steps in order to prevent mistakes in the future. However, most worriers and ruminators take this to the extreme and worry about a hypothetical future that in most cases is unlikely to turn out exactly as you expected it to. You may be dreading a meeting with the boss that she scheduled for first thing Monday morning. Over the weekend you have been ruminating over the meeting: 'Am I going to be fired?', 'Has she found out what I said in the corridor about her the other day?' You go over and over in your head all the possible scenarios of the meeting and before long you have dismissed yourself. You then think, 'How will I pay the mortgage?', 'What will I do without a job?', 'I will never get another job at this level at my age'. Your thoughts begin to spiral out of control, you don't sleep well and by Monday morning you look and feel emotionally and physically exhausted.

This is not a good time to have a meeting with your boss, especially as your defences are weakened. Many times when situations like this occur, the anticipation is often worse than the end result. For example, you go into the meeting and the boss, to your relief — and to some annoyance as you have been worrying about this all weekend — congratulates you on the work you have been doing and asks you to join her on a project she is working on. This is a hypothetical situation, but many similar stories have been told to me over the years by people who ruminate about work and have difficulty switching off and unwinding during their free time.

Rumination, if left unchecked, leads us into an imagined hypothetical future of 'what ifs'. Some people call this counterfactual thinking. Counterfactual thinking literally means 'contrary to the facts', and can also refer to situations/events that may happen in the future; such thinking also revolves around what might have happened but did not. For the most part, these hypothetical futures rarely come true; as we all know, it is impossible to accurately predict the future. In essence, counterfactual thinking requires us to hold two or more different realities or alternatives that may or may not turn out to be true. When we ruminate we often test these in our minds in order, we think, to reduce the emotional stress.

Thoughts are just thoughts

The question is, how do we stop ourselves from ruminating about work issues? Essentially, this is what the book is all about. Each chapter provides different strategies that will help in this process, and unwinding from work will become more natural after you adopt these techniques. This chapter, however, presents a cognitive perspective of switching off from work. As stated above, unfortunately there is no switch we can flick to stop us thinking about work issues; however, the main thing is to get your mind off your ruminative way of thinking so that the thoughts fade away and don't play on your mind. It is like gradually turning down a loud piece of music. It is no good simply trying to shout louder above the music. Keep telling yourself that thoughts are only thoughts, and you are more than your thoughts. You can control your thoughts just as you can control other aspects of your life. If you pay attention to a ruminative work-related thought when you would rather not, the thought and emotion associated with that thought will get a hold of you. Acknowledge that thought but don't pay attention to it. Let it go and it will fade away. There are a number of key principles you can follow.

Tip 1: Change your thinking from 'why' thoughts to 'how' thoughts.

One of the key principles of cognitive therapy is that thoughts are only thoughts. Thoughts cannot harm us unless we act on them. We cannot change what has happened in the past and we cannot fully anticipate what will happen in the future. What causes distress is the emotion that is associated with the thought. In terms of rumination, psychologists distinguish between two classes of thoughts: why thoughts and how thoughts. Why thoughts are the type of thoughts that occur to us in response to an upsetting event. For example, 'Why do negative things always happen to me?' Thinking with why thoughts can be a common reaction when something goes wrong; it is human nature to grieve about past failures, loss or injustice. It is good to let these thoughts out now and again. However, this style of thinking is not very helpful in the long term and can lead to further negative thoughts. How thoughts, on the other hand, can be seen as more helpful thoughts. For example, 'How can I get out of this mess?' When you notice yourself asking 'why, why, why?', you need to change your style of thinking from 'why' to 'how' thoughts. For example, instead of repeatedly asking yourself 'Why was I so stupid?', 'Why do negative things always happen to me?' ask yourself 'How can I make this situation better, how can I stop it occurring again?'

Tip 2: Take note of when you ruminate.

Some people find that certain situations or certain people cause them to have negative ruminative thoughts about work. Look out for and become aware of what triggers these thoughts. Is it one particular person at work? If it is, try to avoid them for a while. This will help but it is not good to avoid the cause of your stress indefinitely. It is important not to take this strategy too far. Don't get obsessed by actively seeking out the times you ruminate;

just be aware of when and where they happen. If you find they are triggered by a certain place, at a certain time or by a certain person, you can take steps to avoid them. Be wise to your thought patterns and when you notice them don't be negative. Simply say to yourself, 'Ah ha, here I go again', 'I know where they lead to', so take action and distract yourself. By doing this, you will feel more in control and it will be easier to take action before your thoughts get a chance to control you.

Tip 3: Engage in activities that promote positive thoughts.

Learn to distract yourself from the thought (see chapters 10, 11 and 12). Do something you enjoy. As Roald Dahl says in *Charlie and the Great Glass Elevator*, 'A little nonsense now and then, is cherished by the wisest men'. A very wise piece of advice for all ages!

Tip 4: Accept the situation and try to look at it objectively.

You have to accept what is going on and look at the problem objectively. Imagine that you were talking to a friend who was sharing a similar experience to you; what would you say to your friend in a similar situation? Would you say that this may sound bad but it is really not as bad as they think it is? Is it really necessary to be worrying about such and such when there are more important things to worry about? The aim of these techniques is to remove you from the emotion and feelings associated with the situation and look at it objectively. This is easier in some situations than others, but, again, with practice this technique will become more familiar and you may actually find yourself offering advice to others.

Tip 5: Distinguish between have/must to, to want to or would like to.

Sometimes people create unrealistic expectations of themselves and others: 'I must have this' (to be successful, to be a good person), 'She must do this for me' (or she is not my friend). You believe if you fail at something you fail as a person. Such thoughts and beliefs impose inflexible demands on you that are not logical or rational, and do not allow any other options. For example, 'I must sleep for eight hours every night (or I can't function)', 'I have to succeed (or I am a useless person)', 'I must not fail (if I do I am a failure)'. Not everyone can be the best so you need to allow for the possibility of other forms of thinking. If you have a problem at work or something doesn't go as planned, this doesn't mean that you will automatically not succeed in the future. Inflexible, rigid thinking will almost certainly lead to ruminative thinking where your thoughts go round and around. It is good to have dreams and goals in our lives, but sometimes we need to be more flexible and change our style of thinking. So next time you find yourself saying 'I must have this', say instead, 'I want to, or I would like to have this'. For example, I would like to sleep for eight hours a night; I would like to finish this piece of work by next week.

Tip 6: Don't overanalyse everything.

Many professional bodies/learned societies today emphasise the need for self-reflection. We are told we need to reflect on every area of our work. When we finish a project, we should write down what went right and what didn't go so well, and then work out why, in order to prevent the negative and increase the positive. This type of analysis appears to make sense but I am afraid it has led to more and more anxiety, cynicism and depression. Sometimes things don't go as planned for reasons seemingly out of our control. Imagine a lecturer delivering her favourite lecture. Most times she has very good ratings of student satisfaction but one day she finds it doesn't go so well and she receives poor satisfaction scores. In her attempt to improve, her natural default method is to self-reflect, but she now over-self-reflects and draws the wrong conclusion. She rationalises that it must be something she has done wrong, and that she is a poor lecturer; and then, not finding anything in particular to change in her lectures, she starts changing things that don't really need changing. The result is that she becomes more nervous and obsessed about her teaching, and her performance suffers, leading her to become more stressed and depressed. Instead of over-reflecting she could have waited to see if the next batch of students reported similar low-satisfaction scores, or even asked one of her colleagues to sit in and observe her. The truth is that it was just this particular group of students who were unresponsive.

John

John is a sixty-three-year-old physics teacher with twenty-seven years' teaching experience and is two years away from retiring. He has worked at the same school for twenty-five years. He likes teaching and believes he is a dedicated teacher. Most years one or two of his pupils are accepted to study at Oxford or Cambridge University. On the whole he is respected by the pupils. The school operates a peer appraisal system and each teacher has yearly classroom observations. This is something he doesn't mind as he normally receives good feedback. However, in his recent assessment John's teaching was judged to be below standard. He didn't even get a satisfactory pass. He thought he had been unfairly judged by the observer – his head of department was being overcritical. He also questioned the validity of the observation process, as he thought it didn't reflect what normally goes on in class. To make matters worse, his observer had only been teaching for six years.

John started to take the feedback personally and came to the conclusion that maybe she was right and he really was not that good at teaching; it had really shaken his confidence, especially as he had always considered himself to be dedicated to the school. He overanalysed each lesson and then tried to follow a prescriptive lesson plan. Not surprisingly, he found his teaching was becoming more 'mundane and woody', and he became too anxious. He started to dwell on his teaching behaviour which led to him being preoccupied with his performance and it became something he just couldn't get out of his mind.

To some extent his action and behaviour can be considered quite normal – everyone ruminates or dwells on their problems – and sometimes this can be helpful because it motivates us to change and reach a solution; however, it can become excessive: 'Why did I deserve this (especially after all my years of teaching)?' instead of 'How can I make my teaching better?' or 'How can I get a better grade?'. In reality, John went from being a really competent, engaging teacher, to an anxious wreck. Consequently he kept getting poorer and poorer feedback, and as a result of being trapped in this vicious circle of thinking he was eventually diagnosed with clinical depression.

Tip 7: Focus your attention only on the things you can control.

Most people like an element of control in their lives, and some people seek more control than others. If you are one of these who likes complete control you will need to modify your style of thinking and let go occasionally. You can never have complete control over your work and home environment; this is neither possible nor healthy. You need to develop more flexibility in your life and learn to accept that it is perfectly fine to let go once in a while and go with the flow!

9
Express your emotions

'The best way out is always through'

Robert Frost

In this chapter I introduce a simple but very effective writing exercise that has been shown to improve physical and psychological health in countless studies in people who have experienced stress or trauma of some kind. If you have experienced something unpleasant at work, or you are being emotionally affected by something that has happened to you or is happening to you at work, and your mind keeps going over and over trying to deal with the issue, or issues, please try the technique suggested in this chapter. The basic idea of the exercise is to release and let go of emotions associated with a particular unpleasant event or experience. Approach the procedure with an open mind and follow the instructions below completely. You may find the exercise a little strange, as some people do when they first encounter it, but, believe me, we have had some spectacular results using it. I must admit that I, along with some of my colleagues, was very sceptical about this technique when we first encountered it but we have become converts after seeing some impressive results.

Let your emotions out

The technique of expressing one's emotions through writing as described in this chapter has now been developed into a standard procedure. This involves writing about an emotional or stressful topic for twenty minutes a day for three consecutive days. As simple as it sounds, this is basically all there is to it. However, this technique has produced some very impressive findings. Expressive writing has been shown to produce beneficial effects for a range of issues, including reducing anxiety and depressive symptoms, lowering blood pressure, reducing the effects of post-traumatic stress disorder and increasing immune function. It has also been shown to be very good at stopping people ruminating about work issues, and this is why I have included it in this book. A note of caution before you start: you may not experience instant results — although many people find the exercise therapeutic in itself — but you should notice changes within a month and these will continue.

The exercise

Choose three consecutive days when you can set aside twenty minutes every evening, when you can be quiet and you know you will not be interrupted. Switch off your phone and your PC so that there are no distractions.

Day 1

On day 1, I would like you to write for twenty minutes about your deepest thoughts and feelings about work. This might be a stressful situation at work that continues to bother you. It could be something that you find difficult to talk about and makes you feel upset, but you keep thinking about. It should be an experience that you have not shared too much with others. When you do this exercise, I would like you to 'let go' in your writing, say how you really feel. You could think about how the experience has affected you in the past, present, or how it may affect you in the future. Once you have finished writing you can put your script in an envelope and shred it at a later date or simply shred it there and then.

Day 2

On day 2, I would like you to follow the same instructions as the previous evening. If you wish you can write about the same topic as the previous day or a new one. However, the topic needs to be related to issues at work. Again, really let go and explore the thoughts and feelings associated with the event. After twenty minutes stop writing and put the sheet of paper in an envelope, as above.

Day 3

On day 3, follow the same instructions as on days 1 and 2. Again, you can write about a previous topic or a new one, just as long as it is something that is bothering you about work. As before, really let go during the writing. After twenty minutes put the sheet of paper into an envelope, as above.

What do people say?

And that is all there is to it. As I say above, you may or may not get instant results, although some people do find the act of writing about an upsetting issue very therapeutic. Below are actual responses from people who have completed this exercise with us.

I found this exercise very interesting. I realised my writing went a lot deeper than I had expected and I found myself reflecting in new ways and drawing different comparisons than I had previously done.

This exercise happened at the same time as quite a tough period in my work so there were a lot of raw emotions around already and this exercise has in fact helped me to process some of that. For example, today (day 3) I've come home from a tough day at work and I've had a tension headache all day but actually it has lessened over these twenty minutes of writing and I do actually feel calmer and more confident.

It was interesting writing about similar and connected things on the three days and relating back to what I had thought about previously – the writing on days 2 and 3 helped me to think about day 1 as well.

I found the pressure of needing to fill this almost as stressful as thinking about work! It felt like homework hanging over my head! Having said that, once you are sitting down to write it is surprisingly easy and twenty minutes goes very quickly. I think that writing about work is like de-stressing with colleagues at the end of the day. It is an opportunity to vent about things that are bugging you and once you have done it – it feels much better – cathartic in fact!

Actually, I rather enjoyed it. I used to write a daily diary years ago and found it most therapeutic.

How does it work?

We don't fully understand why or how it works. The method was originally developed by an American psychologist, James Pennebaker. Initially it was developed from working with victims of trauma and it was thought that writing about the event was a cathartic exercise, a purifying or cleansing of one's emotions. Also, some have suggested that it works in a way similar to counselling. Talking about an emotional or upsetting event has long been known to help people cope with negative experiences. A problem shared is a problem halved. We do find in our research that the people who show the greatest benefits tend to report the use of more emotional words when writing, therefore supporting the cathartic hypothesis. Another possibility is that expressive writing works because it allows people to disclose distressing work-related incidents without the fear of conjecture, or ridicule, or of being judged. It is also likely that expressive writing allows people to develop a coherent narrative, thus allowing incidents to be processed and stored more effectively.

However, this does not fully explain how it works. Research also suggests that by repeatedly verbalising the stressful experiences a form of habituation occurs, whereby the memory of the event becomes stored in part of our long-term autobiographical memory. Sometimes during therapy patients may inhibit information and choose not to disclose feelings because they fear being judged or may be ashamed of their past. However, by writing the event down, people tend not to feel so protective and are therefore more able to express their feelings and emotions. It has also been suggested that expressive writing helps us to restructure our thoughts in a more positive way. Notwithstanding, none of these explanations seem to explain fully how or why it works. The simple truth is that we don't really know how this works, and in one sense it doesn't really matter how it works. We drive our cars without fully understanding the mechanical processes involved. Nonetheless, we have had lots of testimonials from people who have used this exercise and found it very beneficial!

10
Distract your mind and fill the void

'Man is so made that he can only find relaxation from one kind of labour by taking up another'

Anatole France

Consider the following. It is now the weekend; all the pressing domestic and household tasks have been done. You have made no real plans as you have had a busy week. You have been looking forward to a lie-in at the weekend, and then taking it easy for the rest of the day. You want to relax, and, let's face it, you have earned the right to.

You wake up — possibly earlier than planned — and have a leisurely breakfast; so far so good. After breakfast you may switch on the TV or read the paper to keep you up to date with the news. At first you find a couple of interesting stories or programmes that keep your brain occupied, but then you begin to get a little edgy and your attention wanders. When this happens your mind will inevitably pay attention to what has been your most recent concern. If you have been working on a project, thoughts surrounding the project will invariably pop into your head. This is especially true if it is something you are really interested in, or you have been waiting for people to send you the information you need to complete the project. We tend to perform this type of behaviour if we have made no concrete plans and therefore we allow our minds to wander back to work because there is nothing to distract our thoughts. As your mind wanders back to work, you may then start to do something work-related just to pass the time, such as checking emails. I use emails as an example but it could be any work-related activity. When you start looking at emails one of two things normally happen. You start reading them, opening the attachments, and before long an hour or so has passed and it is as if you had been at work. Alternatively, you scan them briefly, but don't deal with them and close your computer and walk away. However, when you do this the contents of the email may play on your mind and end up doing so all weekend. In my view this is a wasted morning. Successful people know their time is a precious commodity. Once time has gone, it has gone for ever. Checking emails at the weekend is a very inefficient way of working.

In this and the next chapter we will discuss the need to find activities to distract us from our work-related thoughts during our free time in order to fill the void — the hole left when we are not working. Some ways may work for you better than others. All take a degree of practice and you need to find the activity that suits you as the mind can be distracted in many different ways.

Without direction the mind wanders

We often overlook the use of time. The notion of time has been with us for so long we frequently overlook its importance. We all feel we use time well, but I suspect we are just kidding ourselves. Those who get more done are often simply better at using their time. In a later chapter I discuss the importance of maximising your working day and giving your full attention to the task. This chapter is concerned with how you plan your leisure time, what you do when you are not working. It may seem counter-intuitive, but one way to stop thinking about work issues when not at work is to do something. Simply doing nothing, just sloping about the house, is not really going to help you unwind. In fact, unless you are really physically fatigued, sloping around the house or lying down watching television actually makes us feel more tired. From 5.30 on Friday evening to 9.00 on Monday morning, there are sixty-three and a half 'potential' leisure hours. However, let's say you need to sleep for twenty-four hours (unless you have a lie-in), which leaves thirty-nine and a half hours, and this is not counting the time you need to get yourself dressed and ready for work on Monday morning. Therefore, don't let leisure time be eroded: plan your weekends and fill the void to stop your mind wandering.

Distract your mind or it will wander off by itself

We all need to distract ourselves from time to time. Our brains are remarkable. A human brain weighs between 1,300 and 1,400 grams (2.87 to 3.1 lb). Our brains are made up of around eighty-five billion neurons (cells that transmit information via electrical and chemical signals) but no one is really sure about the exact number. Neurons are connected to each other via synapses, so there are literally billions of connections. It is these connections which are responsible for our sense of thought, which give to the notion of our mind. Even though thousands of psychologists and neuropsychologists research the workings of the brain, we still don't really know how the mind works. But we do know that the brain is the most delicate and efficient computer known to man. When working well, our brains can make millions of calculations with relative ease. Within our brains our minds have created brilliant art, music, sculpture and literature. The human brain is clearly a remarkable organ capable of producing many great things.

As in life, however, there is a trade-off. We also know that our minds are rarely idle and they are also greedy in that they need constant stimulation. There is a lot that goes on below the level of consciousness, and our brain, if not stimulated by our external surroundings, will start to wander off. It is like a ship that needs a navigator. Without a navigator it will drift. Even when we sleep, at our most rested our minds still crave stimulation and this is possibly why we dream. Dreams are, I think, used by our brains to fill the void. During waking hours, however, we need to control or distract our brains. We do this quite easily at work by paying attention to what we are doing at any given moment. However, when not at work, and when there is nothing particularly appealing, stimulating or motivating to capture our attention, our minds tend to wander. Invariably, as you already know by experience, it frequently wanders back to work-related issues. It is therefore important that we all find a distracting activity when not at work.

Children can take your mind off work

Distraction can take many forms and sometimes it's not obvious which activities are the best distracters. An example of this was a study I was involved in a few years ago.[1] In this study we were interested in the concept of family roles on health and in particular blood pressure. We fitted individuals with a device called an ambulatory blood pressure monitor which measures blood pressure and heart rate while an individual goes about his daily business. In the study we divided the sample into three groups: one group were single and had no children, the second group had a partner but no children and the third group were parents who were married or living with a partner but had at least one child at home. We expected that single people would show the greatest reduction in blood pressure over the evening, but this is not what we found. The greatest reduction in blood pressure was observed in the parents. There were no gender differences, and the findings could not be attributed to variations across groups in terms of subjective feelings of job stress, physical activity or location during measurement. Thus, having to look after a child appeared to facilitate recovery (as indicated by a reduction in blood pressure, suggesting that attention to family issues (e.g. making dinner, interaction with a child) can distract someone from their work-related thoughts.

In the aforementioned study we did not actually assess whether people were thinking about work, but we recently completed an additional study in which we asked people to complete an online survey about how they unwind from work. We didn't measure blood pressure or any other physiological variables. Interestingly, the results were supportive of our previous study. The parents with young children reported less difficulty switching off from work, compared to those without young children. Also, and against what I expected, parents with young children reported less acute and chronic fatigue, and had better wellbeing and were happier in life.

Why does having children help the recovery process? The first study was conducted with schoolteachers but the occupation of the participants doesn't really matter. The answer appears that having young children distracted their parents from work-related issues during the evening. Having to cook dinner, and sitting down interacting with family over a meal, etc., automatically switches attention away from work and by doing this it helps people to unwind. Thus, by performing these activities the parents were distracted from work, and work-related activities, and consequently they were able to disengage. Conversely, for the single people there was nothing to interrupt their work-related thoughts, and so they continued to think about work issues. The point is that in addition to not working during our free time we need to find something to distract us, or, conversely, to hold our attention so that we don't think about work.

Distraction works by focusing our attention on something other than what's going on inside our heads. We can distract ourselves in many ways: for example, by listening to music, taking exercise, reading, going to the cinema, socialising with friends, or watching an interesting programme on television. Psychologists distinguish between active and passive distraction tasks. An active distraction task might be playing a sport, interacting with your children, rock climbing, or dancing, for example, while a passive task might be watching television. It is no great surprise that research has found that energetic activities that involve mental engagement — that is, paying attention to some activity — work better as distracters than passive ones; although it is not as clear cut as some television programmes can be more engaging than others.

Don't be too leisurely about your leisure

One way to distract our minds is to plan our leisure days and bring some structure to our free time. Having a plan also fills the void left by not working or thinking about work. However, in order to do this we need to use our weekends sensibly. A weekend is actually only two days, not counting Friday evening, and if you don't plan and just idle your time away, before you know it the weekend is over and you have accomplished nothing. Occasionally, a slothful weekend is fine if you are really exhausted and need a rest, but try not to be idle. If you remain idle at the weekend, and sit around watching mindless television, channel hopping, looking for something interesting or stimulating, you are more likely than not to find neither and end up watching any old nonsense (although you convince yourself it is interesting). If you do nothing, you will feel lethargic and it will take a while for you to get going on Monday. Sometimes, when people have a lazy Sunday, they find it more difficult to sleep that evening, and therefore feel unrefreshed come Monday morning. According to Laura Vanderkam, author of *What the Most Successful People Do on the Weekend*:

> 'Success in a competitive world requires hitting Monday refreshed and ready to go. The only way to do that is to create weekends that rejuvenate you rather than exhaust or disappoint you.'[2]

Plan your weekend as you plan your work

It doesn't really matter when you start planning your weekend but I would advise you not to leave it to the last moment before you do so. You could start planning in the middle of the week but perhaps it is better to allow yourself a few minutes this weekend to plan for the next. Don't be too obsessed about planning every minute away: I suggest you also build in some slack. The important issue is for you to have fun and enjoy your weekend!

Don't wait for the ideal opportunity. I think it was Churchill who talked about escape hatches. When people don't really want to do anything, and don't want to accept blame, they give themselves an escape hatch. 'I can't do the garden today because it is likely to rain'; 'I would love to read a book but I just don't have the time'. Don't just think about the day — make it happen and plan ahead. No plans ever work 100 per cent so build in some slack.

We unconsciously think about the weekend as time away from work. Interestingly, if you ask people to rate how career-oriented they are, they will give a different rating depending on the days of the week. Studies have shown that people will report being more career-focused at the beginning of the week and less at the end. What's more, they do this subconsciously. This suggests that people are already winding down for the weekend.

Many people today believe that what happens outside work is as important in terms of work performance as all the planning, skill developing, etc., is done at work. The person who has a fulfilling and meaningful life outside work is normally very productive and successful in their professional career. Those who live a boring, dull existence away from work — the types who choose to idle in front of the television — appear to be just as idle and unenthusiastic at work. I guess this is not too surprising; after all, it is the same person with the same personality traits. A conscientious, determined person at work will be just as conscientious in other aspects of their lives. It is perfectly acceptable to relax and do nothing, so you can rewind and charge the batteries. If you do find your mind wandering, however, give yourself something to do. If you find yourself on your own and don't feel like doing any jobs around the house or garden, go for a walk. If possible, switch the phone off, or, better still, leave it at home, especially if you think you may be tempted to check work calls or emails. Some people now have two phones, one for work contacts and one for family and friends. Don't be too harsh with yourself. It is OK if your mind starts to think about an issue at work; as I said in an earlier chapter, sometimes this helps us to be creative. Productive and successful people make time for leisure pursuits but they also use their free time (evenings and weekends) to reflect on work. As stated in chapter 5, thinking about work issues outside work is not always harmful and thinking about work issues in a relaxed, detached manner helps us to see the bigger picture. Weekends are ideal times for us to reflect and recharge our batteries.

A distraction activity doesn't have to be a physical activity

Thinking and being preoccupied about work-related issues may be interrupted by both planned and unplanned distractions. As stated above, we can distract ourselves in many ways but the best distracters are those that capture and hold attention.

While it is not possible in most instances to spend all of our non-work time on activities that promote recovery, it is important nonetheless to budget in some 'active' distraction activities during your leisure time. There are many different activities people can pursue to relax and switch off from work-related thoughts. The actual activity in itself is unimportant: therapeutically, the real issue is whether it is sufficiently engaging to distract your attention away from work. The key is to find something that is absorbing, preferably something you enjoy, and that takes your mind off work. For some people it may be doing the crossword over a coffee or a glass of wine; for others it could be baking, ballroom dancing, doing a pub quiz or sailing. In pursuing activities our thoughts are directed to what we are doing at that particular moment. Your activity becomes your preferred thought. It is really like a form of meditation. If you are absorbed in an activity you will find that time passes quickly. You will wonder where it went.

Distraction works by focusing your mind on something other than your symptoms and what's going on inside. There are different methods of distraction, and sometimes you may find that you are not in a place where you can absorb yourself in your preferred activity. In situations where this occurs you can use a visualisation technique. In each case you need to keep your mind focused for at least three minutes before your symptoms will start to alleviate. Here are some of the more commonly used distraction techniques.

You could try to visualise a pleasant scene in your mind in which you felt calm and happy — or focus on an object, like a flower or your favourite car. Really concentrate on it, bring it to life in your mind. Having a 'bridging' object such as a photograph or souvenir from a happy time means that, when you look at it, it can help trigger positive thoughts and reduce anxiety. Try doing a puzzle or sums in your head, or counting the number of red doors you see on your way home, or imagining what the people you see do for a living.

Make the weekend expand

One final tip to make the most of your weekend, and stop yourself thinking about work. In *What the Most Successful People Do on the Weekend*, Laura Vanderkam extols the virtues of scheduling something fun or meaningful for Sunday evening to stretch out the weekend and to focus the mind. I think this is very good advice and something I have been advocating for years. Going out for a drink, a meal, or going to the theatre or cinema on Sunday evening makes perfect sense (so long as you are not out too late). Sunday evenings seem to be quite relaxed and most places are quieter than on Friday or Saturday evenings. Eating out on Sunday evening is great, as most restaurants are quieter, so you never feel hurried and you don't have to worry about cooking Sunday dinner. By going out and paying attention to your fellow diners and your surroundings, your mind will be focused on the present, instead of thinking about all the work you need to do on Monday morning. Why not expand the weekend and enjoy a Sunday evening out with your family or friends?

I think you will agree that, at the end of a working week, most of us look forward to the weekend. The weekends offer us the chance to recover from work-related demands, and the people we work with, and the possibility of pursuing interests and activities outside of work. However, don't let your weekend slip through your fingers and distract yourself by filling the void. Top performers, in any field, know that the secret of their success is to use time wisely and I am not only talking about paid work time; this includes the weekend. An ideal restorative weekend needs planning. Most people do not consider the weekend in any detail until Friday, and many leave it until they roll out of bed on Saturday morning. Learning to create restorative weekends requires thinking about weekends differently. Think about it as a time to do what you want to do and use the time wisely.

11
Develop a hobby

'Today is life — the only life you are sure of. Make the most of today. Get interested in something. Shake yourself awake. Develop a hobby. Let the winds of enthusiasm sweep through you. Live today with gusto'

Dale Carnegie

In the previous chapter I stressed the importance of filling the void — finding something to do to stop your mind wandering and, more importantly, to stop you wasting your leisure time. In this chapter I discuss the importance of hobbies. Finding a pastime that you really enjoy is an excellent way to relax and unwind.

Develop a hobby and become a top performer at work

If you need convincing about starting a hobby, read on. Surprising as it may sound, the importance of having a hobby was demonstrated in an interesting study by Satu Uusiautti and Kaarina Määttä[1] from the University of Lapland, in Finland. Uusiautti and Määttä conducted interviews with eight top workers. A top worker in this context was someone who had received an award for being 'employee of the year'. As may be expected, such people were characterised by working hard, being motivated for success; those individuals also had a positive view on life and on developing a friendly social atmosphere at work. Interestingly, employees of the year also talked about the significance of having a good hobby. Hobbies were used as a way of unwinding from work, and to counterbalance the effects of working hard. Some hobbies could also influence work. For example, one top worker in the study was a priest who enjoyed both reading and writing novels and poetry in his free time. Not only did pursuing this hobby enhance his wellbeing as it helped to direct his thoughts away from work; it also indirectly aided his work as it enhanced the writing skills that he used in his everyday work. Thus, having a hobby does not suggest that you are more interested in pursuing your own selfish interests; a hobby is not only a resource to aid unwinding but can be a positive conduit to feed into your daily work. This is true of many hobbies, such as becoming fit, reading or even playing golf.

We all need a hobby

Why are hobbies important? A good hobby is one that is pursued for its own sake. It doesn't really matter what the end result is, so long as the person enjoys the experience. Moreover, it is the experience that is the reward — a person finds pleasure in doing the activity, the motivation for doing an activity is internally driven and not motivated by any external force, e.g. a person does not restore vintage cars in order to make money, a fisherman does not sit on a canal bank just to catch fish. It would be a lot quicker and easier to buy fish from the supermarket. A good hobby is one that is pursued for its own sake. As we noted in chapter 5, philosophers and psychologists use the word 'autotelic' to describe such a process. Thus, a good hobby is one in which a person can lose himself. A good hobby is one in which we can fully immerse ourselves. Our conscious mind is not infinite. If we are paying full attention to a hobby, there is little or no room left for other issues at work or at home. Thus, a good hobby not only distracts us, it also controls and demands our attention. The art is finding a hobby that captures our attention without too much mental effort.

Why not build a wall or paint a picture?

It is well known that Winston Churchill spent much of his time at his beloved country house, Chartwell, which he enjoyed restoring. He famously built the wall that surrounds the garden. Another of Churchill's hobbies was painting although he didn't actually take it up until he was in his forties, doing so in times of personal and political adversity. He found painting a great distraction and he is quoted as saying, 'If it weren't for painting, I couldn't live; I couldn't bear the strain of things.' He went on to paint more than 570 pictures. Sir Alex Ferguson, the former manager of Manchester United, is reported to have developed an interest in golf as a way to relax and escape from the pressure of managing a successful football team.

Develop your passion

A hobby is an activity you pursue in your spare time for enjoyment or relaxation. A hobby is time for yourself; it is *your* time. We have so many commitments in life — work, shopping, washing, getting the children ready for school, etc. — that it is also good to do something that we want to do. This may sound selfish, and to a degree it is, but you need to remember this is your life, not mine, not your neighbour's. I have spoken to so many people who have started a hobby late in life and wish they had started a lot earlier.

It is important to find a hobby for which you have a passion. A hobby can enhance our knowledge and wellbeing and give more meaning to our lives. Practising a hobby gives us a sense of achievement and makes us feel more in control. Hobbies relax the mind and are an excellent way of unwinding. People who regularly engage in a hobby are less likely to report stress, and less likely to suffer from anxiety, fatigue or depression. A hobby is personal to you; you do it because you find it enjoyable not because someone else thinks you should be doing it. A hobby can be a solitary activity, or it can be a social experience if you become a member of a club. The key is that you do it to fulfil your needs, not someone else's. Thus, the perfect hobby is one that is rewarding to you!

What hobby should I pursue?

I cannot recommend which hobby you should pursue — hobbies have to be a personal choice. Hobbies are therapeutic because they distract the mind to focus on something other than your symptoms or your work. Even physical hobbies such as playing badminton or football help to relax the mind as both require you to concentrate and pay attention to what's going on at that particular moment. A hobby that requires concentration will distract the mind better than one that does not. However, you will find that once you become interested in something, for example gardening, you will become absorbed in the activity. Choosing an active activity — one that involves some mental engagement — is not clear cut as some seemingly passive activities, such as watching television, can be more engaging than others. However, any activity that seizes and holds our attention is a good distractor.

Develop an interest

You may think that you have no interests. In his excellent book *The Magic of Thinking Big*,[2] David Schwartz discusses ways people can develop interest in and enthusiasm for almost anything. The basic premise is that you need to gain knowledge and become a bit of an amateur expert in the area. He calls it the 'dig-into-it-deeper' technique. You can use the 'dig-into-it-deeper' technique to develop enthusiasm for almost anything; all you need to do is to find out all you can about a certain subject. For example, you may decide that you should grow a few vegetables; many people believe growing your own is more environmentally friendly and home-grown food is more tasty and satisfying. The first year you clear a patch of ground and put in a few potatoes, lettuces and so on. Before long you find yourself checking to see if they are healthy and not being attacked by slugs or snails. You may start talking to friends or neighbours about the vegetables you grow, and start watching programmes on the subject. You may find that Christmas and birthday presents seem to reflect your new interest as your friends start to associate you with gardening. Before long, you realise that people are beginning to seek your advice — suddenly you are an amateur expert in growing vegetables. Once we start something our natural curiosity takes over.

There are literally thousands of potentially interesting activities to pursue. You just need to choose one for yourself. I can assure you that once you start paying attention to something it will become interesting, and you will then feel the benefit of doing something you really enjoy. Do something you find pleasure in. If your passion is painting, paint — paint whatever you want, however you want to. Don't be put off even if people criticise you. Remember you are not painting in order to be the next Rembrandt or to please your friends; you are painting because you like to do it.

'I have no time for hobbies'

When I talk about this in my seminars people frequently say to me that, while they agree that activities/hobbies are a good way to relax post-work, they have no time to pursue a hobby. It is an excuse I hear time and time again — 'I have no time for a hobby, I am just too busy', 'I have no time for a hobby, I am just too tired', 'I have young children so there is no time for me to do anything for myself'. It is as if they have no control over any aspect of their lives, and evidently this appears to be the case for many people. I have even heard some say they will start a hobby when they retire. Why wait until you retire? You may have less money, be less agile and less likely to learn. Those people who do have a hobby seem always to find time or make time for it. There is never the right time for any hobby, so you need to make the time; be organised and plan your week. If it helps, make a date with your hobby and schedule it in your calendar. When you take up a hobby that you really enjoy you will find time for it, and you will schedule your time better. This may mean getting something finished on time at work so work doesn't spill over into the evening, and you will find that you need to manage your home life better. You will probably notice that you don't spend so much time in front of the TV.

Thus, by pursuing a hobby you will have to become more organised. Once you start a hobby, and you set a time when you pursue it, your family and friends will quickly come to respect that this is your time.

Another excuse I hear is that people have no one to pursue a hobby with. Maybe you are new to an area or you have lost contact with friends because you have been too busy at work, or your friends are simply not interested in trying new activities. In such cases, I recommend you go out by yourself. I know this may sound harsh, but if you wait until your friend is free you will wait for ever. There are many activities you can do on your own, for example, going to the theatre, or joining a sports centre. If you are not sure where to look for a new hobby, try the ads in local shops or free newspapers. Your local radio is another good resource for finding recreational activities, as is the library. Maybe you will come across a wine club or book club you never knew existed, or find an advert about learning to play an instrument. There may be a card/games night at your local pub — or one not so local if you worry about being seen on your own. There are also many adult educational courses, most of which are not only an excellent way to learn a new skill and to broaden your mind, but are also a fantastic place to meet new people.

Having a hobby to pursue will get you out of your daily routine, and help you relax. A good hobby will break up your week and give you focus at work. You will feel relaxed and less fatigued, and your mind will be clear. Many hobbies may not appear that interesting at first, coin collecting, for example. I am not a great coin collector but I became interested in it by chance after going into a shop to get out of the rain while waiting for a meeting in London. At the time I didn't know anything about coins so I chose the cheapest one on display; it turned out to be Roman. The shopkeeper wrote down the date the coin was in circulation and with a bit of detective work I discovered that it was from the Valentinian dynasty and dated from between 364 and 392. It was minted in honour of Flavius Valens who was promoted to the rank of Augustus in 364. Valens spent much time campaigning against the Goths and Persians, and died in a ferocious battle near Hadrianopolis in 378. From this chance experience I have now added another twenty-five coins to my collection and continue to add to it. Even if you pursue a solitary hobby, you will quickly meet like-minded people who may share ideas, tools, etc., with you; some of them may even become friends. Hobbies also give us an identity. You never know, you might even unearth a hidden talent you didn't know you had.

Two out of three small businesses started as hobbies

Many people have turned their hobby into a successful business. The reason for this is that in order to run a successful business you need to be passionate about what you do or sell. If your business is about selling you really need to like selling. If you have your own car repair workshop you need to be passionate about cars. If you love jewellery, your designs will reflect your passion. It stands to reason that if you are really passionate about a product or a service, this will shine through when you speak to customers or clients. People are more likely to want your services if they see that you will go the extra mile for them. You cannot hide passion.

One final point: you may think that having a hobby is not that important at this time of life, as you are concentrating on your career and don't have the time. This may be true on one level, but remember you will not work for ever. If your work is your life, once you are forced to let it go there will be a big void to fill. Not only are hobbies good for counterbalancing work demands and a very nice way to spend your free time — concentrating on something other than work — but at the end of your career a good hobby could be surprisingly rewarding!

12
Leave work at work

'I believe that being successful means having a balance of success stories across the many areas of your life. You can't truly be considered successful in your business life if your home life is in shambles'

Zig Ziglar

As obvious as it seems, the first thing you need to do in order to help you switch off during your leisure time is to stop working. By working, *ipso facto* you are thinking about work and preventing yourself from switching off and relaxing. More importantly, you are also delaying and reducing the time available to relax and unwind. True, some people can switch off quite easily once they have finished working, but most of us need a certain amount of time to unwind. This varies; for some it may take only a few minutes, for others from three to five hours to unwind, and a small number of people don't really switch off at all.

It takes on average between half an hour and an hour and a half to unwind during the evening

I am not suggesting that you never work beyond your contracted hours. There are times when we all need to work late in the evening and sometimes all through the night in order to get the job done. Ironically, I am writing this chapter during the twilight hours! Indeed, I think it is nonsense to suggest that work and home are either mutually exclusive or have to be mutually exclusive domains. If you are at home but find yourself in a creative and productive mood, why not carry on working? By doing so you may be able to save time or produce something you would not otherwise have done. Working can also be sufficiently rewarding in itself, and a source of pleasure. However, constantly working long hours is not generally considered good for health and wellbeing, and in fact it is very bad for our health. As reported earlier, long work hours pose a serious health risk. It is not just the stress or the demands that work places on us but the indirect effects of not exercising, not following a healthy diet and not sleeping that contribute. None of us are superhuman.

Take the example of Michael Eisner. In 1984 Eisner became the CEO of Disney. At the time, Disney was experiencing financial difficulties (to put it mildly) and was haemorrhaging money. During his stewardship, Eisner transformed the corporation and presided over an ambitious expansion plan. From having an initial market value of $2 billion, in 1984, Disney's market value flourished to $75 billion in 1997. A remarkable turnaround, most would agree. Michael Eisner was a tireless, competitive worker, putting in many long days, and on the surface appeared very healthy. However, in 1994 he started to experience pains in his arms and chest and was diagnosed with heart disease, leading him to undergo immediate open-heart surgery. Prior to the heart attack, Eisner had been working longer and longer hours and had difficulty sleeping, something he normally had no problem with. He also gave up exercise and stopped following a healthy diet. The rationale for stopping exercising was that he was simply too busy. The reason I have included a few lines about Michael Eisner is that no matter how intelligent, driven and successful we are, we all need to take time to unwind and look after ourselves.

Leave work at work

Leave work at work. It is as simple as that. When you leave work, stop working. I have conducted a number of workshops on ways to manage stress and on helping people to unwind from work. One of the first questions I always ask my attendees is: do you work in your leisure time? I'm amazed that there is always a very high percentage of people who work way beyond the call of duty. Sometimes people don't realise there are alternatives to working excessive hours. Imagine you are a professional athlete. You could not train all the time: overtraining can lead to poor performance, loss of motivation and an increased risk of injury. Similarly, you can't expect someone to be mentally fresh and give 100 per cent at work if they don't allow themselves downtime. If you are continually working, you will not switch off and unwind.

In 2009 we reported the findings of a study in which we conducted interviews with middle-level managers who were selected on their responses to our measure on their inability to unwind post-work.[1] One of the interesting findings to emerge between the groups was that the high ruminators would never stop working; they were, as we say, over-committed to their job. Over-committed individuals work outside their normal contractual hours, or if self-employed, will work nearly all the time. In this study all our high ruminators described how work monopolised their life, which blurred the boundaries between work and home. For example, Jeremy, a self-employed builder, when asked how many nights he works late, said:

> '… all the time, unless I'm going house-hunting [incidentally, this is still work] – which is quite stressful in itself. But I normally work fifty, or maybe up to fifty-five or sixty hours per week a lot. I am constantly juggling a number of projects, organising people for different jobs, or writing quotes and invoices.'

This may seem quite noble, but all the people we interviewed complained that they could never switch off from work – they simply surrendered themselves to their job. Nearly all of them reported working between fifty-five and sixty-five hours a week. Some of those interviewed were also starting to display the early signs of fatigue and were beginning to wonder how long they could keep up the pace.

This live-to-work philosophy was very much in contrast to the low ruminator's work-to-live approach to life, for example:

Peter's (low ruminator) comments:

> '… even if I've got loads of stuff, I just get to the point in the day where I'm like, right, I'm going home and I don't care, I'll just walk out, go home, and have a good weekend and then just get back on when I come back in … everything's urgent but it's not that urgent, I kind of go with the philosophy that nothing's life-threateningly urgent, so … there is pressure there, but I know I can sort of manage or tackle things as they come in and sort it out.'

Simple small steps are better than giant leaps

As I said above, obviously there will be times when you need to work late in the evening, sometimes all evening, and even throughout the night if it is absolutely vital to complete an important piece of work. However, if you find yourself working all the time and you don't enjoy the process, you need to change your working pattern. There are a number of ways you could do this.

First, you need to reduce the amount of work you do or the number of hours you work during the evening and weekends. You can do this by going 'cold turkey' — and immediately stop working any evenings — but this is probably not the best or easiest approach. I suggest you begin slowly and gradually reduce the extra hours you work. Pick an evening next week or the following week to start with, so that you can begin to prepare yourself not to work. Don't worry: you can still work some evenings, but also plan to have evenings when you don't work and, importantly, don't answer your phone (if it's a work phone), or check emails. I have produced a timetable, which you can use to schedule your leisure activities as you would your work (see chapter 13).

If you work every evening, if only for a couple of hours, over the next couple of weeks decide which evening you will not work at all. Not even to check your emails. Put this in your diary so that you don't take work on. You can post an out-of-office response so that no one will expect to hear from you if you are in the habit of responding promptly. Mark the evening you plan not to work in the chart, and stick to it! Use this time to relax, spend time with your family or socialise, but don't work. After a couple of weeks, and once you begin to enjoy and look forward to your work-free evening, try a second evening. You may have to reduce your workload a little to accommodate this extra time at first, or you may even find that you are starting to be more productive at work so that you don't need to work in the evenings any more. It is strange how 'work expands to fill the available time for its completion', as C. Northcote Parkinson once observed. If we have ten hours in order to complete a report, it normally takes us ten hours; but if we only have eight hours, somehow we manage to complete it within that time. It is good to have boundaries and deadlines as these tend to focus the mind. We all need deadlines in order to prevent work expanding, and, let's face it, the consequences of missing a deadline do spur us on.

'Everyone needs deadlines. Even the beavers' Walt Disney

Even if your work does not have an imminent deadline, it is nevertheless beneficial to set yourself a target (more on this later). On those free evenings don't worry too much if your thoughts occasionally drift to work matters. Indeed, as you take control, you may find that your thinking becomes more focused as you begin to have clarity of thought. You may be engaging in some leisure task when suddenly you find the solution to the problem that has been nagging you at work. Think of Archimedes in his bath. This is when thinking begins to switch from being predominantly negative in content — what we called affective rumination in chapter 5 — to problem-solving pondering. You cannot force this style of thinking and creativity, and, moreover, you don't want to stop this process.

As I have said, many of our most creative thoughts come to us when we least expect them, typically when we are not working. For example, considered by some as one of the principle founders of chemical structures, the German organic chemist Friedrich August Kekulé had been struggling to determine the structure of benzene.

He knew that it contained six carbon atoms but he wasn't sure what the structure would look like. He had been working on this problem for a while without making progress, when one night he had a lucid dream. The dream was about six snakes forming a ring by eating each other's tail. When Kekulé saw this, he made the connection to the chemical structure of benzene. There are various versions of this story, but Kekulé himself said that this vision came to him only after years of studying the nature of the carbon bonds.

You may also have been in the habit of working all weekend and you need to stop doing this. I suggest you take at least one day off at the weekend, unless you are working on an important project or working on one of your own. OK, if you feel you need to catch up with work from the previous week or need to plan for a Monday morning meeting, or even spend time on some serious reflection, then allow yourself to work. You can work on Saturday mornings, but don't work all day. As reported earlier, if you know that you will be working on Saturday, don't be surprised to see work waiting for you when you wake up on Saturday morning. I bet that if you were about to go away on your annual holiday you would have found time to do this work during the week. It is amazing that we can cram so much in when we need to.

If your job requires you to be creative or solve problems, not working during your weekends will, ironically, make you more productive and creative. People have told me that they were initially sceptical when I first told them to break their habit of working during their leisure time, but once they got used to not working they became more productive, more creative and happier at work. They also said they became more engaged and focused at work when they were at work, and were less inclined to moan and gossip. Incidentally, I think gossiping should be avoided. If you can't be open with your colleagues you will never be a full team player. Successful people don't gossip, they simply get on with the task in hand.

If you examine the habits of very successful people who have excelled in their careers, you will see that there are some who constantly work, but the vast majority will say that their best ideas came to them when they were not actively thinking about the issue. Their greatest inventions or insights occurred in what scientists call their epiphany or eureka moments — they occurred when they were least expecting them to occur.

13
Setting aims and goals in life

'You are never too old to set another goal or
to dream a new dream'

C. S. Lewis

How many of us plan our evenings? Not many. I am always amazed that, when I speak to people (especially those who find it difficult to unwind mentally after work), how many of them don't make plans for their leisure activity during the week. Most people come home, have dinner and then work or sit in front of the television until bedtime. Actually, a lot of people do both; they will sit down but either still work while watching TV or think about work. Unfortunately, if we are not careful this becomes a habit. The aim of this chapter is to encourage you to become more proactive in your leisure time and take control.

What did you do on your free evenings last week?

Copy out the table below and take a few minutes to make a note of what you did on your evenings, say, last week or the week before. What is a typical evening for you? I suspect a lot of time involves doing the essentials like having dinner and clearing up afterwards; but once this was done, did you work or think about work issues, read a book, go to the gym, or did you watch television because you felt too exhausted to do anything else? You can use the table below or devise your own format. If you cannot remember what you did, you can use this as a diary for next week. Write down what you do each evening. It is best if you can work out roughly how many hours or minutes you spent on this task. It is important that you do not change your usual behaviour, and that you are honest with yourself. We will call this your present self.

What did you do in your evenings last week (present self)?

	6 p.m.	7 p.m.	8 p.m.	9 p.m.	10 p.m.	11 p.m.
Monday						
Tuesday						
Wednesday						
Thursday						
Friday						

What would you like to achieve in life?

Now take a few minutes and think about what you would ideally like to achieve in life, especially during weekday evenings. We will call this your ideal self. If you are happy with your evenings and you don't wish to change anything this is fine, but read on nonetheless. People have their own goals and aspirations. That may be to complete an evening course, do more socialising or simply spend more time with your family or partner. It could be redesigning the house or garden, decorating or becoming more self-sufficient by growing your own vegetables. If you always wanted to get into physical shape, now is the ideal time. If you always wanted to know more about wine, it may be the perfect time to find a wine club to join. If you always wanted to participate in your community you could think about doing charity work one evening a week. Maybe you wanted to start ballroom dancing? Why not give it a go? The list of possibilities for leisure activities is endless:

Indoors

Acting, board games, bookbinding, bowling, calligraphy, candle making, card playing, chess, collecting (coins, stamps, etc.), cooking, creative writing, crocheting, dancing, embroidery, flower arranging, home brewing, knitting, model building, playing a musical instrument, pottery, quizzes, reading, sculpture, sewing, singing, sketching, squash, taekwondo/martial arts, woodworking, yoga

Outdoors

Archery, astrology, backpacking, basketball, beekeeping, bird watching, bodybuilding, cycling, fishing, football, foraging, fossil hunting, gardening, golf, hiking, hill walking, jogging, kayaking, metal detecting, mountain biking, mushroom hunting/mycology, paintball, photography, polo, rafting, rock climbing, roller skating, rowing, rugby, running, sailing, shooting, shopping, skiing/snowboarding, sub aqua, surfing, swimming, wine tasting/making

Whatever you choose, do not think about it in any detail at the moment, just write it down. Writing things down is always better than trying to remember them.

What you would like to do in your evenings (ideal self)?

	6 p.m.	7 p.m.	8 p.m.	9 p.m.	10 p.m.	11 p.m.
Monday						
Tuesday						
Wednesday						
Thursday						
Friday						

Put your plan in motion

Next look at your lists and decide which goals you would like to pursue. To start with choose three things from the list that are reasonably easy to accomplish. I would start with something easier at first but this is up to you. Once you have narrowed it down to three, I want you to select one goal to work on first. Let's pick an easy one, as in going to the cinema with a friend/partner once a week. One night, instead of working, checking emails, watching television, or doing what you normally do on week nights, why not download a film or, even better, go to the cinema? If you have a partner, make it a night when you go out together. This need not be too expensive if you choose the night when perhaps there is an offer on. If you enjoy watching movies, why not make this a regular occasion, and plan to go at least once a month. You can go on your own, but if you have a partner or a group of friends who enjoy movies, even better. Even if going to the cinema is not your idea of fun, you could join a book group, take up golf, or cooking, etc., the point being that you need to find an activity or hobby that you enjoy, and one that you do on a regular basis. As you do something on a regular basis, sooner or later it will become a habit — and you know how difficult it is to break a habit — and you will find that your mind is not so preoccupied with thoughts about work, so you will find it easier and easier to switch off. Your mind has only a limited capacity, so by focusing your energy on another absorbing activity your attention will be directed away from work and on to that activity. There will obviously be occasions when your mind wanders, but you learn not to pay too much attention to these thoughts and to redirect your thoughts to the activity at hand.

Plan next week

Each weekend, say, on a Sunday, plan what you would like to achieve in your free time the following week. Do this with one eye on your long-term goal. Write it down. Below is an example but you will need to create your own plan. I am not saying that you should never watch television and I am certainly not saying that you need to cram as much in as possible over the week, but start by planning one or two activities. This is my list below. You will also see that I have deliberately left some free time; these are the times when you are free to do whatever you wish. You can work in the evening or check your emails — we will gradually wean you off this practice — and there are times when it is good to do absolutely nothing. Once you start planning your week you will feel more in control, and you will start to acquire a sense of achievement.

Making more of your leisure time

Do not set too many goals. If you do so it is unlikely you will be able to achieve them all, and then you will become frustrated and regress back to your old self. Also, don't try to do too much within one goal; build in some free time, otherwise you'll become exhausted. This is the complete opposite of what the exercise is for. You have a much better chance of achieving your goals if you simply allow yourself to aim for one or two easier goals in the first three months at least. Your planned evenings will soon become the norm. Once you see that you are beginning to take more control of your life you could then start to think about bigger goals. Obviously, if it is a big goal you will need to break it down into smaller sub-goals to make them manageable. For example, if your goal has been to build a garden shed, you could choose a sub-goal of clearing the ground and laying the foundations. Think about how other goals relate to your long-term goal and try to incorporate other activities that lead to your long-term goal.

Monday	Quiet night in with the family
Tuesday	Quiz night with friends
Wednesday	Swimming, then quiet night in
Thursday	Evening course
Friday	Get all the housework done or go out

Implement your plan

As stated earlier in this book, unwinding is an action-oriented process, and we need to apply self-initiated activities in order to recover from work. Therefore success can only be achieved by action. The final step is to implement your plan. This is the hardest part. It is very easy to set goals; the difficult part is sticking to these goals, especially when the going gets tough. The mind is a marvellous tool; it can be very creative, it is a very good problem solver, but it is also very good at stopping us reaching our goals. It does this by putting obstacles in our heads. You may hear yourself saying, 'This will never work, I'm far too busy', 'I haven't got time for this', 'When I come home from work I'm far too tired to think about going out'. Don't let such thoughts put you off.

You need to stick to the plan. Try it next week or the following week. Give yourself a starting date. It is probably not advisable to start immediately. Also, feel free to modify your plan if you decide it is not really what you want to do. A friend and I decided to try a new activity once a month, something we had not done before, just to see if we enjoyed it or found we were quite good at the activity (e.g. golf, go-kart racing, badminton, etc.). This would be part of your plan — to try something new once a month.

It is important that you aim to stick to the plan as much as possible. It is inevitable that things crop up from time to time, and there will be occasions when things do pile up or something occurs that is completely out of your control. You may find, for instance, that you are invited out on the night you had planned to do something in particular, or you may find that you have an important deadline to meet at work. It is imperative that you stick to the plan as much as possible in order for your behaviour to become a habit, but it is also essential that you do not become a slave to the plan. The whole idea of this exercise is for you to take more control of your free time, and try not to get distressed if things don't always go the way you envisaged. Life has a strange way of not behaving and throwing up the unexpected. This is OK, and part of the richness of life; so long as you remain as faithful to your plan as possible you will find that you become more in control and less focused on work during your leisure time. You should also find that you are more engaged during the day when you are at work.

A final thought: a life filled with different, challenging, thought-provoking experiences has to be more rewarding and worthwhile than one that involves being a passive recipient of vast amounts of mundane, passive entertainment.

14

Let yourself
relax

'The secret of health for both mind and body
is not to mourn for the past, worry about the
future, or anticipate troubles but to live in the
present moment wisely and earnestly'

Buddha

I n 2010 the American Psychological Association reported the results
of a survey that found 70 per cent of Americans perceived work to be
a 'significant' or very significant cause of stress. When we experience
stress we demonstrate stress reactions that manifest themselves in
a number of different ways. I think such stress reactions can be
classified under four headings: physiological, behavioural, cognitive
and affective.

Physiological reactions include increased heart rate and blood
pressure, elevated lipids, as in cholesterol, endocrine, cortisol and
reduced immune response, especially if the cause of stress is long

lasting. Behavioural factors can be any behaviour that is bad for us in the long term, including smoking, drinking alcohol excessively, eating too much unhealthy food, and/or not exercising. Cognitive reactions to stress manifest themselves as cognitive errors, as in forgetting the name of someone you have just met, and affective reactions to stress are experienced as anxiety and depression, for example. Stress at work can also spill over into the home and family. The study by the American Psychological Association also found family responsibilities to be stressful, with 58 per cent reporting that this was a significant cause of stress. It appears there is a lot of stress about, and it is clear that we all need time to mentally and physiologically disengage from life stressors and spend time on rest, recuperation and recovery activities. You need to relax. How many times have you been told this or heard it said to someone? The word 'relax' is a verb that comes from the Latin 'relaxare', which simply means 'to loosen'.

People who have difficulty unwinding from work typically report two main issues. Firstly, they find it difficult to relax, and, secondly, they can't escape from their work-related thoughts — they can't stop thinking about work. In this chapter I will introduce an exercise that, if done well, should almost guarantee that you will quickly learn to relax, switch off and abandon work-related thoughts post-work: it's called the mindfulness body scan. Practising mindfulness is an effective way of reducing tension and aiding unwinding, and in particular I find the body scan an excellent technique for helping people relax and unwind. Mindfulness meditation promotes awareness of feelings and sensations, the need to focus attention on these sensations and the notion of being in the present and in a state of acceptance. I am sometimes asked if there is a difference between mindfulness and meditation, and at the basic level it is difficult to tell them apart, as they both centre on breathing, relaxation and attention. In this chapter I will use the terms mindfulness and meditation interchangeably.

Meditation is not just for hippies

When people think about mindfulness meditation they may conjure up the image of someone (a long-haired hippy type, maybe) sitting crossed-legged, chanting in a cold room in order to reach some truth or utopia. Another perception is that meditation takes years of practice. Both of these are misconceptions. It is not true: people don't spend years and years practising something before they see the benefits, and most of us are not the long-haired, woolly jumper types. Some people may be searching for enlightenment but most of us use mindfulness meditation in order to relax because we find it beneficial. Another misperception is that people are too busy to meditate, and think it would take too much precious time before they gain positive results. On the contrary, meditation has almost instant results. And once you have the basics, meditation can take as little as ten minutes per day. Moreover, once mastered, you can incorporate aspects of meditation into your everyday life and find benefits throughout the day.

What is mindfulness meditation?

Mindfulness meditation is really the art of mental self-control. Learning to meditate is an excellent way to gain control over your mind and thoughts. Meditation is therefore a brilliant skill to have in order to free the mind from work-related thoughts. There are many different ways to meditate although they all share a common premise as they are all concerned with how we are thinking and feeling inside. The mind can be quite demanding and can even be our own worst enemy. Everyone experiences irrational thoughts from time to time. We may wish such and such to happen, and we all have insecurities, and feel emotional, and at times we may act in haste and then come to regret our actions. The art is not to act on impulse but to enhance the way we think in order to create mastery of our lives. One of the aims of meditation is to teach people to focus on the here and now, and not to think about the past or the future.

Thus, done correctly, meditation will give you back the feeling of self-control; as they say, it can quite literally 'change your mind'. You need to train your mind to work with you, not against you. Your mind is one of the most powerful processing devices on the planet so we need to use it effectively. At the end of the day, a disturbing thought is only that — a thought. As stated earlier, a thought in itself does not hurt us; it is how we react to the thought that causes us to experience stress. Meditation has been shown to have a number of health benefits, including lowering blood pressure and improving sleeping quality. Studies have even shown that brain structures and gene activity change in response to practice. Also, people who frequently meditate report fewer headaches, experience less fatigue and tension and greatly improve their efficiency at work. We have demonstrated in a number of studies that practising meditation, even a few minutes a day, is one of the most effective ways of reducing stress and facilitating the unwinding process. Why not give it a go?

My experience in working with different people over the years is that the people who tend to do the best with these techniques are those who are open-minded and give it a go. One aspect of mindfulness is to train us to learn to observe our thoughts. Mindfulness allows us to be aware of negative thoughts, to notice and label them, and then let them go. We don't have to process the thought any more. Thoughts can appear and disappear from our consciousness as clouds across the sky. You may ask how is it possible to concentrate on one specific thought when there are so many distracting thoughts. Most people are able to concentrate on a specific thought for a short while, especially if it is an intense thought. I would bet you have experienced days at work when time passes so quickly the day is almost over before it has begun. When you are working and focused on an interesting project, this is called flow; you focus on a piece of work and your attention is completely absorbed by it.

However, as soon as we relax, fears, anxieties and negative thoughts pop into our head. Sometimes when you are watching television you may find yourself suddenly confronted with a work-related issue, such as 'Did I send that email?', 'Did I upset my boss today for not doing x?' It may appear that we have little control over our thoughts, and when we are in a certain mindset we tend to experience unpleasant images or thoughts. We may find we have become obsessed by the same thought or desire. This can torment us endlessly and we often feel, irrationally, that we are being tortured for some past sin. We are continually bombarded with stimuli from the external world and we may find ourselves constantly making judgements: I don't like ... that reminds me of ... and so on. Some thoughts seem so strong they even affect our judgement. So, our basic task is to learn to clear our mind.

The mindfulness body scan

For this exercise, find a quiet place to sit or lie down where you are unlikely to be disturbed. Make yourself comfortable and give yourself a minute or two to settle. You can place your thumb and forefinger together or just place your hands to one side. Now breathe naturally and focus on the various sensations when you inhale and then when you exhale. Focus on your stomach rising and falling, and notice the sensation of the air coming in and out of your nose. As you inhale, cool air is drawn into your nose, where it is warmed and humidified. As you exhale you may notice the slight difference in the sensation. Try to breathe through your nose, but remember to clear your nasal passages beforehand (your nose contains hairs whose job it is to act as a filter). If you can't clear them, don't worry, just breathe through your mouth. Don't try to rush the exercise, but just breathe naturally. This is such a simple but very effective technique. Once learnt, you can practise it almost anywhere, on a bus, train, or even when you are nervously waiting to be interviewed for a job. The more you practise, the more you will find it easier to relax.

We tend not to pay too much attention to our breathing and take it pretty much for granted. However, we can harness the effects of breathing. As we breathe we take in oxygen, which gets taken up into our bloodstream, and we release carbon dioxide as a waste product from the heart and lungs. It is believed that defective breathing can actually contribute to certain negative conditions such as anxiety, tension, headaches and fatigue. It is therefore important to learn to breathe correctly.

Typically we demonstrate two breathing patterns: chest or thoracic breathing, or abdominal or diaphragmatic breathing. Chest breathing is a form of shallow breathing. When we inhale our chest expands and our shoulders rise as we take in the air. Breathing is often irregular and rapid. We tend to do more of this type of breathing when we are stressed or anxious. When we breathe using our chest we tend to take in too little oxygen and carbon dioxide builds up in our body and this can lead to feelings of light-headedness, heart palpitations and shortness of breath.

Diaphragmatic breathing is slower and more rhythmic breathing in which air is inhaled deep into the lungs as the abdomen expands and the diaphragm contracts. Air is then exhaled as the abdomen and the diaphragm relax. You can tell how you are breathing by placing one hand on your stomach around the waistline and the other on your chest. Now notice when you breathe how your hands rise. If you notice that your abdomen rises more in relation to your chest, you are breathing diaphragmatically. If your abdomen doesn't change that much in relation to your chest you are more likely to be shallow chest breathing. Your aim is to learn to do more diaphragmatic breathing, and less chest breathing. You will achieve this only with practice. You should find that as you do more diaphragmatic breathing you will start to feel more relaxed and less tense.

The mindfulness approach focuses on increasing the acceptance of thoughts and feelings by focusing our attention on the present moment. Try not to think about the past, or the future; just try to focus your attention on the present. The principle is to observe whatever thoughts or images that come to mind, but not to process the content of the information. Observe the thoughts in a non-judgemental way.

Once you are comfortable focusing on your breathing you can begin to explore other parts of your body. Start with your left foot, gently examine the sensations in your toes and ankle, and then gradually work up to your knee and hips, and then explore the right leg. Observe and note any sensations you experience while practising the body scan, but try to let go of these sensations and thoughts before moving on to the next area of your body. Also try to keep still while doing the exercise. Once you have explored the lower half of your body you can then start to explore the upper parts. I will not go into more detail here. There are many websites that provide free mindfulness body scan audio exercises, and if you enjoyed the exercise it may be worth checking these out.

Whenever you finish a relaxation procedure give yourself a couple of minutes to gradually return to normal. This is particularly important if you have your eyes closed during the exercise. Deep relaxation will result in a fall of blood pressure and therefore you need to allow yourself a little time to adjust. You may experience faintness if you suddenly stand up after a session. At the end of the session gently shake your legs and arms and rest for a couple of minutes. Notice how peaceful and relaxed you now feel. When you are ready, get up and carry on with your daily activities.

Once you have become familiar and experienced with the mindfulness approach, you could try to be mindful in other aspects of your life. For example, how many of us eat without really paying attention to the sensations we experience in our mouth? Pay attention to the smell of the food, the texture as well as the taste. You can also become aware of the sensations when we swallow food: the sensation of your muscles in your oesophagus as it contracts and relaxes while pushing the food down to your stomach. Ironically, you may even find that you eat less when you become more mindful of the food you eat.

Important! Relaxation techniques should not be used if you are suffering from hallucinations, delusions or you experience other psychotic symptoms. If in doubt, seek the advice of a qualified medical practitioner before you start the body-scan exercise.

15
The notion of a favourite place

'To sit in the shade on a fine day and look upon verdure is the most perfect refreshment'

Jane Austen, *Mansfield Park*

In the brilliant US hit comedy *The Big Bang Theory*, Sheldon Cooper, the genius scientist whose life seems to be ruled by logic and scientific principles, does have an emotional side — he has to sit at the end of the sofa — his special favourite place. For Sheldon, no other seat will do. He tries to justify why he needs to sit in this place and no other by claiming that it gives him a perfect view of the television, that it is not too hot, not too cold and not draughty; but the real reason why he likes sitting there is that he just feels comfortable there, and he can relax. It is his favourite place.

Find your favourite place

Each of us may have a particular place or places we find restorative. A favourite space is a place where we feel comfortable and relaxed. Particularly following a period of high demands and stress, a favourite place allows for the renewal of one's coping resources, contemplation and reflection. A favourite place is typically somewhere you have developed an emotional attachment to over a period of time. It could be your favourite place because it is associated with a previous positive experience, but, equally, it could be a favourite armchair, a certain part of your garden or even a park bench. A favourite place is anywhere that allows us time to gather our thoughts and help us to develop and maintain our identities. You may have a favourite armchair, a place to sit and watch television. It could even be in your garden shed, or your customary spot on the beach. There is no one place I would recommend to help you recover from work and unwind. A place can have meaning for you for a number of reasons. You may associate a certain place with positive past pleasurable experiences or emotions — a beach, a park, a holiday destination, even riding your horse — or almost anywhere where you experience positive emotions or cognitions.

A favourite place does not necessarily mean an exotic beach. It does not necessarily mean a place of solitude — although a favourite place for someone could be going on a retreat — as your favourite place could in theory be the football ground where you enjoy watching your team play. You may even have more than one favourite place; it could be your chair and also a place in the garden that you find particularly relaxing. It may be somewhere you find fascinating and stimulating such as an art gallery, music venue or theatre. It could even be having a quiet coffee or drink on the way home from work. The point being that you use that particular space for yourself; it is your space, a space to regulate your emotions, a place to relax, calm down and clear your mind. People use favourite places not only to escape and unwind from work but also to escape from other stressors of life. A favourite place gives us respite from the pressures of living. If you work in a busy office or you have to be sociable all day at work, you may seek solitude in the evenings and sit down for a short while in your favourite place. On the other hand, if you primarily work by yourself your favourite place may be the local pub or bar where you can interact with people.

The scientific explanation

Psychologists will argue that people use a particular place for self- and emotional regulation. Self-regulation is a term used to refer to our abilities to control our behaviours and moods. The aim of self-regulation is to keep inner tension as low as possible, thus maintaining a favourable level of self-esteem. It is taken that people primarily prefer pleasant psychological states more than unpleasant ones. For example, an individual may exercise in order to maintain a level of fitness and body shape in order to maintain a positive self-image. People high in self-regulation are more likely to succeed in tasks and their goals.

Self-regulation primarily involves the control of thinking, attention, concentration and emotion. All these aspects play an important role in unwinding and recovering from the demands of work. As you may come to realise, most of the chapters in this book offer advice and strategies you can use to regulate your emotion and reduce your thoughts about work issues. Pursuing artistic and cultural activities, socialising, and spiritual/religious life can potentially enhance life satisfaction, and investing in these types of activities is likely to help you mentally unwind from work.

Rachel

Rachel is a busy mother of two who typically works six days a week, and on top of this does most of the housework, as, in her words, 'if not, it would not get done'. Her favourite place is the beach. Just sitting or walking, it doesn't matter. By being at the beach she knows she will not be able to do any work, check emails, etc., but also, because she is a busy mother, she knows that when she is at the beach she will not get distracted by having to do chores around the house, by friends knocking on her door, and thinking what she needs to do for dinner.

Give yourself some time to reflect

Make a date with yourself each day to spend a little bit of time just being. Many of us spend our days trying to do too many things — running from meeting to meeting, trying to solve a problem, dealing with angry clients — and then coming home to housework. Many people complain that life today does not seem to afford them the time or the opportunity for personal reflection. Perhaps this is true, and this is why we need to make our own time. Each day set yourself at least ten minutes just to sit quietly pondering and reflecting on things. Create your own oasis of calm. This is not the time where you do formal meditation exercises. It is up to you when and where you do this but find somewhere you can reflect and think without distraction, without the radio or television on; perhaps during your lunch break or sometime during the evening. At first this may seem a little difficult but after you have been practising the exercise for a while it will start to become habitual. You will just do it. You will notice also that you become calmer and think more clearly. You will be able to see what needs to be done at home and at your work; what is important and what is not so important. This exercise is not designed to make you introspective with regard to all parts of your life, merely to help you unwind and gather your thoughts — in order to give yourself some breathing space.

16
Park that thought

'The highest possible stage in moral culture is when we recognize that we ought to control our thoughts'

Charles Darwin

Something that I fully recommend is that you can avoid thinking about an issue until it is convenient for you to do so. The idea behind this exercise, which I call 'park that thought', is that you can do this until you are ready to deal with it. Think of this as the way you would normally plan an activity during your day, for example, cutting the lawn or checking emails. You can decide to cut the lawn, check your emails now or later; either way, they will still be there when you go back to them. Similarly, you decide when you will allow yourself time to process the thought in the same way as you decide when to pay attention to a particular piece of work or check emails, for example. You don't allow the thought or issue to intrude into your head space until you are ready to deal with it. This is easier if you have something you have to deal with first; for instance, you say, 'I am overwhelmed now, but come back to me later'.

Some people find this a lot easier to do than others. It is nonetheless a skill you can develop and use once you have mastered it. The act of acknowledging the thought but delaying it seems to help you subconsciously, as you know you will return to the thought soon. When you do return to the issue you may find it is not that important, and you will certainly have saved yourself a lot of emotional stress and anguish over the day.

Unfortunately, unless you are very skilled in parking that thought it is quite difficult to do, especially if the thought is an emotional one, something that has clearly upset you.

There are two different ways you can use the parking approach for work-related worries. The first is purely emotional; and the second is more analytical and focused on problem-solving.

Thoughts are just thoughts

Parking for emotional, upsetting thoughts

If there is something truly upsetting or distressing and you can't deal with it at this particular moment, park the thought and set a time for dealing with it. Write the time down as if it is an appointment in your diary. If the thought comes into mind before your appointment, remind yourself that you have planned to deal with it later on. Write in your schedule two periods in the day when you can devote yourself to your worrying thought. You need to give yourself ten to twelve minutes for each.

When it is the appropriate time:

- Make sure that you will not be disturbed during the exercise. Find somewhere quiet where you know you will not be disturbed; switch off your mobile phone.

- Next, start to think of the issue. When you start to worry about the problem, don't think about finding a solution to it. Do not say to yourself that these worries are irrational and you are being silly.
- Try to generate as many negative thoughts about the issue that is bothering you as you can.
- Don't try to look on the bright side of things. The aim of the exercise is to let all the negative stuff out.
- Allow yourself to become anxious and emotional during the exercise.
- Keep thinking about the worrying thought for the full ten minutes and return to the thought even if your mind wanders.
- Once the ten minutes are up, let the thought go and practise a relaxing breathing exercise for two to three minutes and then return to a previous activity or start a new activity.
- If the thought comes back into your mind, remind yourself that you have another session planned to deal with it later on.

How it works

The exercise works on a number of levels. Firstly, once you have let your emotions out you will feel a lot calmer and more relaxed. You will also find that you are not being swamped by your emotions. You will begin to have clarity of thought. Letting your emotions out releases the build-up of tension and frustration associated with the cause of your stress. The world always seems calmer after a storm. Don't worry if you start to cry during the exercise; crying is a good way to let your emotions out. One survey showed that nearly 90 per cent of people feel better after a cry. Also, don't worry if you don't cry; the exercise is not meant to make you cry but if you do during the exercise that's OK.

Secondly, time is a good healer, and by parking a thought you let time take over and often, once you return to the thought, it doesn't seem so distressing. You may also have built up some resistance to the thought in the meantime, so you are better equipped to deal with it; moreover, I think by letting time pass you are not adding fuel to the fire as you would normally do if you tried to process it instantly. Instead of instantly acting on something, you let the impulse pass and by doing so you stop the vicious circle of rumination developing. In addition, by parking the thought you have shown yourself that you have control over that thought.

Thirdly, the exercise works as the emotional stress associated with the thought loses its power. You will find that the more you do the exercise, the more difficult it will become to complete the ten minutes. Over a few days, you should find yourself running out of ways to express the emotion, and the potency of the emotion will diminish. Eventually the thought will just seem like a thought but without the emotion attached to it. Instead of feeling anxious when you re-experience the thought or emotion, you will become used to it and get bored by the exercise. Finally, over time your body will develop a natural resistance to the cause of the stress. This is a very effective exercise that can be used to park non-work-related thoughts. However, if you experience other more serious thoughts please consult a health professional.

Imagine that you had an early meeting with your line manager or a client and they criticised you, unfairly in your opinion. Instead of ranting and raging you think to yourself, 'I am not going to think about this now, I have to deal with another issue first that is more pressing'. In a way this process works because you distract yourself by thinking about something else. It is important that you don't try to suppress the thought — as in the example of the white bear (see next chapter) — as it will only bounce back. You cannot park the thought indefinitely. You will have to let it out and deal with it at some stage. You can choose not to cut the lawn today but it will still keep growing. However, later in the day or evening you start to think about the issue and you realise it was no big deal and your line manager or client may have had a point and was only trying to help. Instead of getting angry at the time, your delay in acting on the thought has not only saved you a lot of anguish and stress during the day, but you have also not upset your boss or a good client.

Parking the thought to deal with it analytically

As in the previous exercise, write the time down as if it is an appointment in your diary, and try not to process the thought if you find it unexpectedly pops into your head before its allocated time. Just remind yourself that you have made an appointment to deal with it later on. Write in your schedule the day when you can devote yourself to the problem. You may need to give yourself a bit more extra time than twelve minutes for each.

When it is the appropriate time:

- Make sure that you will not be disturbed during the exercise. Find somewhere quiet where you know you will not be disturbed, switch off your mobile phone, lock your office door, or find a place somewhere where you will not be interrupted and can pay full attention to the issue (e.g. in the park, having a coffee by yourself).
- Depending on the problem, write it down on a piece of paper and generate solutions. You could do a list of pros and cons. Generate as many solutions as you can via stream of consciousness.
- Now process your solutions.
- Work on the problem from an objective, analytical point of view. Don't let your emotions take over. See the issue from the other side.
- Do you need to get another's opinion? If so, do it.
- If the solution involves compromise and a loss of face, accept it.

If you start to worry about the problem during the day, don't think about finding a solution to it or start processing it. Acknowledge it as an issue but remind yourself that you have set a time later to deal with the thought, and any emotions you experience you will also deal with later.

Karen

Karen works in sales and marketing. Her work is normally well received by her managers and she is frequently praised. During a weekly meeting the sales manager announces that one of the campaigns that is due to launch in a couple of weeks' time is falling behind schedule and needs immediate action to rectify the situation. When Karen leaves the meeting she receives a phone call from her partner, who makes a sarcastic remark about an ongoing problem, and, although clearly upset, Karen chooses to park that issue and any negative thoughts surrounding it, as she needs to focus on the problem in hand. She decides to set aside twenty minutes later in the day when she knows she will have the mental strength to deal with it. In the meantime, Karen is able to get on with her work as professionally and competently as normal.

17
White bears and not-so-quick fixes

'If you don't control what you think,
you can't control what you do'

Napoleon Hill

I n the previous chapters I have discussed a number of effective strategies for dealing with work-related thoughts that you should adopt. In this chapter I will discuss strategies that you should avoid.

Imagine that you are talking to your friend about the difficulty you have in switching off and unwinding from work. Your friend says she has just read in a magazine about a technique that is bound to work — it is called 'thought stopping'. Thought stopping is a technique for getting rid of negative and repetitive thoughts by suppressing them. Whenever you experience an upsetting thought such as 'I must work on that project', 'I'm really dreading seeing my boss tomorrow', 'I really need to close that deal', your goal is to force yourself not to think about these things using a technique called 'thought suppression'. You are encouraged to shout either to yourself or aloud the word 'STOP'.

In the clinical practice patients are also instructed to wear a rubber band on their wrist and each time they experience an upsetting thought they are told to snap the rubber band. Over time this is supposed to reduce the number of times you experience such a thought via a process called conditioning. Unfortunately, over time this only leaves a nasty mark on your wrist as thought stopping in this way does not usually work. Moreover, it actually leads to a rebound effect and makes things much worse. This only makes us try harder to suppress the thought, resulting in a snowball effect. When we try to suppress an upsetting, unpleasant thought we fail and experience the emotional stress accompanying that thought, so we try again even harder. The thought appears more insistent in the rebounding. This is pointless. It is similar to when we are upset and people tell us to 'snap out of it' and cheer up. If it was that easy we would have done it ourselves.

Try not to think about a white bear

There are now many laboratory studies that have demonstrated the futility of trying to suppress such unwanted thoughts. In a series of interesting experiments Daniel Wegner and colleagues have demonstrated beyond doubt that by trying to push unwanted thoughts out of consciousness, people actually make the thought more accessible. Originally a question posed by the Russian novelist Fyodor Dostoyevsky, in *Winter Notes on Summer Impressions* (1863), Wegner asks participants to stop thinking about a white bear. Each time an image or thought of a white bear comes into their mind, the person presses a button or announces that they are thinking about a white bear. Try this yourself. Stop reading the book for a couple of minutes and then try not to think about a white bear. Do this for two minutes and see the results.

In doing this task I bet you thought about a white bear more than once. Now imagine if this was an unpleasant, upsetting or disturbing image or thought you were trying to suppress and not think about. The more you try to suppress it, the more you will experience such a thought and also experience the negative emotional reactions associated with that thought. The emotional reactions manifest themselves in the form of tension, anxiety, etc., and are unpleasant. It is quite obvious from the above example that thought suppression does not only not work, it is also counterproductive in the recovery process.

Thought suppression does not work because each time you try to suppress a thought you have to pay attention to it. You cannot simply decide never to have a memory of an event. Each time you try to suppress the thought you are actually paying more attention to it and therefore making the thought more accessible to consciousness. You have then paid attention to the thought you are trying to suppress. It is like having a direct route to the unpleasant thought. If such a process existed we would never be unhappy. If we were sad or upset we could just drum up a positive thought — hey presto, we are now happy. Unfortunately — though perhaps there is a good reason for this — our brains don't work in this way. There is no magical button or off-switch; we cannot choose with certainty which memory we want to think about at any given moment.

Don't look for a quick fix

To help overcome or tolerate excessive fatigue and stress brought about by not being able to unwind from work, many people seek quick fixes. A headache can be treated with a tablet — although a lot of headaches are caused by dehydration — and drinking water with the pill is in many cases the reason why the headache goes. To give us a quick start to the day we have adopted the habit of having a cup of tea or coffee first thing in the morning or on the way to work. It is amazing how many people you see walking or driving to work clutching a large plastic beaker. The problem with this is that, over time, the body becomes physically dependent on the relieving properties of the substance you have been ingesting. In such cases, instead of increasing your resilience and control over the stressor you become dependent on the drug to stop the side effects or withdrawal symptoms. Take smoking, for example; we find that, as a group, smokers are more likely to ruminate about their work and have difficulty unwinding compared to non-smokers. Smokers often say they need a cigarette to help calm them down and reduce stress and unwind. Sometimes they choose to smoke with a coffee, therefore getting a double whammy of stimulants. What is actually happening to people who smoke or are used to taking sedatives is that, as the effects wear off, they start to become a little tense. If they are experiencing a problem at work, or they have work issues on their mind, these thoughts will intensify.

Using alcohol to unwind

Trudy

Trudy is a public relations consultant working at a leading medical communications company. She works extremely hard in what is a competitive world and she earns a good salary. Trudy is a conscientious, diligent employee who is prepared to put in the extra hours in order to get the work done. She has recently been promoted and her responsibilities have increased. Her job involves a fair bit of travel and she frequently finds herself staying away from home. She often works late in the evening entertaining clients, managing launch parties, or similar events. She has always been very professional at work, and, unless offered, hardly drinks alcohol while she is working. Due to the late nights, and the task of running the events, and the additional responsibility, Trudy was finding it more and more difficult to unwind at the end of the evening. Sometimes it would take her two to three hours to get to sleep. She found sleeping particularly difficult if the project meant she had to work away from home and stay in a hotel for a couple of nights. She started to have the odd glass or two of wine at night to help her unwind and escape the pressures of work. The wine helped to dampen her thoughts about work, and it seemed to slow down her racing mind, helping her to fall asleep. This is not an uncommon story; many people like to unwind with a glass of wine, whisky, or a beer or two, and used sensibly alcohol can be a good relaxant.

Alcohol: a useful tonic but it's not the panacea

I always ask people at the start of my seminars to list ways they have tried to unwind. I have not delivered a single session without someone mentioning alcohol. Following a busy day or week at work — good or bad — it can be nice to pour yourself a glass of your favourite drink, sit down, relax and take a moment to chill and reflect. Even better for taking your mind off work, if you can have fun and share a few drinks with some friends.

Alcohol is an interesting one, and it is good every now and then to have a beer or the occasional glass of wine. As a relaxant, alcohol can aid sleep onset as it slows down brain and central nervous activity, and therefore may appear to be the panacea for switching off from work. Many people have told me that alcohol helps them to relax and get to sleep, as Trudy, in the above case study, found. Although considered a relaxant, alcohol in fact impedes sleep quality, particularly deep sleep that is important for memory, tissue and bone growth, and immune functioning. People who drink alcohol to unwind from work often report waking up feeling tired and unrefreshed. Alcohol consumption is also associated with early morning awakening, especially in middle-aged and older people who may also find themselves waking up in the night needing to go to the bathroom. In Trudy's case, on the mornings after using alcohol to help her sleep, she normally wakes up dehydrated and finds it difficult to get herself going. On such days, work appears more demanding and she struggles to get as much done, and therefore finds herself working later simply to catch up.

Having the odd drink is a very good way to relax and unwind, although it is not something I would advise on a regular basis in order to help cope with the stressors you face. It is all too easy to take the quick option and then run the risk of becoming dependent on alcohol to relax. If you use alcohol on a regular basis you are not actually confronting the cause of the stress, as getting drunk is basically an avoidance strategy. You need to find other ways to help you relax and think calmly about the causes of stress in order to be in the position to equip yourself to handle work demands more effectively. Excessive alcohol consumption can negatively impact your body in a number of ways. Alcohol causes dehydration and decreases coordination, endurance and balance. It can lead to weight gain as many alcoholic drinks are loaded with calories, and alcohol can impair the ability of our bodies to absorb essential nutrients for health. Nonetheless, one glass of your drink of choice during dinner or in the evening can be very good for relaxing the mind. As they say, moderation is the key. It is fine to have the odd drink but, please, if you like a drink, drink sensibly and keep your alcohol consumption under control.

18
Don't be a technology slave

'This is perhaps the most beautiful time in human history; it is really pregnant with all kinds of creative possibilities made possible by science and technology which now constitute the slave of man — if man is not enslaved by it'

Jonas Salk

Work is no longer a place you go to, but something you do or something you choose to do. The development emergence of laptop computers, tablets, etc., and the advent of wireless equipment has made it easier than ever for people to work remotely. There are obvious advantages to mobile working. You can instantly communicate with the office and connect with clients, no matter where you find yourself working. You don't need to be at your desk to check a presentation, you can send emails and texts on the way to meetings and you can keep up with the news if you wish. However, one downside to remote working is that it erodes the natural physical boundary between home and work. Over the years this has become fragmented, and there is now no clear demarcation between the physical working world and the rest of the physical environment.

Conversely, it has also made it difficult for workers to escape from work, to switch off and stop working, as with easy access there is always the temptation to check emails, work on a presentation, check the status of a project, send an invoice, etc. All such tasks are valid and work-related, and in theory they could improve your working life — imagine going to work with an empty email box. However, many tasks we do away from the office are not that mentally challenging, although some obviously are (writing reports, etc.), as most of the time we are just checking emails. We convince ourselves that by engaging in such behaviour this will save us time later on. The problem occurs when such practices become the cultural norm. Even companies that put procedures in place to encourage employees not to send emails past a certain time in the evening find that somehow they keep sending emails. I have even heard of some organisations closing down their server during out-of-office hours; however, this sometimes creates problems if there is an urgent task or people are working overseas. In such cases people resort to the phone and private emails. In order for such a strategy to work it needs buy-in from senior management.

Unfortunately, some people think it shows dedication to their job if they send emails late in the evening, or really early in the morning, and, conversely, it suggests we are not dedicated if we don't respond. I now make it a habit not to respond to emails past 8 p.m. and only on Saturday mornings at the weekends. If you can, stop sending or replying to emails outside normal working hours. Once you start responding to emails this becomes the norm and people will expect you to respond and they will be frustrated and annoyed when you don't.

In order to unwind, switch off your phone

This is a direct quote from a participant in one of our studies. In discussing his use of technology to keep in touch with the office, Stephen, an insurance adviser, said: 'I have a BlackBerry that I use all the time. I use it at home, I use it on the train, I use it on the golf course [laugh], I use it anyplace I have to, I use it on holiday.'

Although this may sound extreme, this is nevertheless a typical response I hear. Many of my clients initially complain that work monopolises their lives, and no wonder if they are continually checking emails as they are continually working. Often people do not make the connection that this is work, because it is something they have done outside work. I made this point earlier, but this is important. Checking emails gives the impression that you are available and that you have nothing else better to do with your time in the evenings or weekends. Consequently your colleagues, your boss or your clients will think it is acceptable to email you after hours and expect an answer. I spoke to one manager who was reprimanded for not replying to her boss and sending him a report by seven o'clock the following morning. He had only sent a request to her at eleven o'clock the previous evening.

It is more common than we realise about people being contacted by work during their vacations. We asked Rebecca, an account manager: 'Have people from work ever contacted you outside your working hours on your personal number?'

> 'Most of them do. When I've been away on holiday they have contacted me, when things have gone wrong and they don't know what to do, and if my boss is away or he doesn't know that they are contacting me when they are not supposed to.'

Even though her boss didn't approve, Rebecca spoke as if this was acceptable behaviour from her work colleagues and that she had no choice.

In order to take control back, the first thing you need to do is demonstrate that you are unavailable. Do not answer the phone and don't check emails after work. This can feel quite empowering. If you have a company PDA, smartphone, etc., either give it back or turn it off during your free time. If you have a company phone, have a second phone for personal calls. How times have changed. Only a few years ago, in many organisations it was not acceptable to receive personal calls at work. Now many people receive work-related calls and texts while they are at home!

I realise this is difficult, so the rule I mentioned in chapter 12 about going 'cold turkey' and abruptly giving up your habit, applies here. It may be difficult to stop checking emails completely or working in the beginning, especially if you have been used to working this way, so start slowly by choosing one weekday evening or a Saturday or a Sunday and don't switch on the PC, PDA or tablet, however tempting it may be. Then, gradually, add another evening and then another until it becomes a habit. If you start with this method you will learn not to be so anxious about missing emails. Your colleagues and boss will soon realise that you are not the person to email at 9 p.m. and expect a completed report by nine o'clock the following morning, and they will respect you for it. They will assume you have something more important to do in your free time and that you have a life. It is unlikely that people will think the worst of you. It is a fact of life that people place more value on something they cannot have, and by showing that you are unavailable it will suggest you are busy doing more meaningful things. If this means you may lose a client, so be it. Do you really need the headache of being a dogsbody, constantly at someone's beck and call until you retire?

Use technology to unwind

In one of our studies we were interested in finding out differences in behaviours between workers who can quite easily switch off from work and those who cannot. We asked the question: what is it that makes some people able to unwind better than others?, and we interviewed high and low ruminators. It was very evident from the interviews that high and low ruminators use technology in different ways. Whereas high ruminators appear to be slaves to technology and will monitor emails during their leisure time, even to the point of taking laptops on holiday, low ruminators are not tempted to connect with work during their leisure. Moreover, we found that low ruminators, those people who switch off quite quickly once work is completed, use technology, but in different ways. For example, these people would phone their friends and family (if they were on the train) or listen to their favourite music or watch movies on their laptops, in order to facilitate the unwinding process and help them unwind on the commute home.

Take control

Don't be tethered to your communication/smartphone: you will become its slave. Switch off the phone immediately you leave work or within an hour of leaving work. Don't be tempted to check emails. Obviously, there will be times when you need to makes calls and work late in the evening if it's necessary to get an important piece of work completed, but make this the exception and certainly not the rule. If you find yourself working all the time and you don't enjoy doing so, ask your colleagues if they share your opinion. Remind people that they will work more effectively during the day if they don't work during the evening. Try to complete your emails during work time. If you tell yourself you will check them later on, they will just get left in the inbox and sit there waiting for you when you get home. It is important to remind yourself that, by turning your phone off and not checking emails during your leisure time, you are not a slacker. By not engaging in work issues you will be more relaxed during your free time and therefore you will have more energy and drive for work, and consequently you will get more done.

Managing electronic devices outside work

Like it or loathe it, mobile technology is here to stay. In this age, however, we will all need to be prepared as to how best to deal with it.

Listed below are simple tips for managing your electronic devices outside of work.

- Switch off the phone as soon as you can when you leave work.
  Get into the habit of refusing to make or/and accept phone calls once you leave work. If you don't answer your phone people will realise they can't get hold of you. If it is really urgent they will normally find some other way of getting in contact. If you feel you can't switch off your phone immediately, make sure you don't take calls or check emails when you are within half an hour of home.

- When you are out with your friends have a technology-free night.
  We have probably all experienced this at some time. We are out with a group of friends, and more than one will continually be checking their phones. This is not only rude (unless it is really important), but you can't really enjoy an evening if your mind is

in two places. If seems as if we have lost our way to communicate. I was once in a restaurant where a middle-aged couple at a nearby table were dining with someone who appeared to be one of their mothers. The pair were constantly looking at their mobiles and texting and their elderly companion was sitting quietly by herself. There seemed little point in her being there. Why not set boundaries and decide to have a technology-free night and interact by speaking to each other?

- When you are at home with your family have technology-free evenings.
  Some people spend more time interacting with their phones than they do with their partner/family. Not surprisingly, studies tend to show that smartphones have a negative impact on close or family relationships. If you are engrossed in your electronic device you're certainly not paying attention to your partner or your children. Discuss with your loved ones boundaries about using electronic devices during the evening (e.g. not during dinner, or after 9 p.m.). This also applies if you have children at home, and it is not good for them to see you always on the phone. Why not switch off the phone altogether and have a good old-fashioned chat?

- Smartphone and tablet use can spoil the moment.
  Imagine you have been looking forward to spending a cosy evening in with your partner. You may have planned to have a takeaway and then spend the rest of the evening watching a romantic film, or just being romantic yourself. During the evening you find your partner looking at his mobile. Instead of giving time to you, he appears to be devoting his evening to something or someone else. How does this make you feel? Angry and resentful, I imagine. Research shows that smartphones and other electronic gadgets can put a dampener on intimacy. By responding every time there

is a bleep or flash on the tablet, you lose the magic of the moment. People used to smoke after sex, apparently; now it appears they check their phones. Switch off all electronic devices or leave them in another room.

- **If you need to check emails in the evenings, do so judiciously.**
Set aside an hour when you can fully concentrate and pay attention to what you are doing. Don't sit in front of the television and try to do two things at once; this is counterproductive. Give the work full attention, finish off in the time you have given yourself and then close down the system and get on with the rest of your evening.

- **Switch off social media sites.**
Some people — and I never know why — appear to be obsessed about telling the world what they are doing. 'I am just going to the pub'; 'I am having a really good time with my friends'. Others feel we need to hear their opinion on everything: 'I don't like xxx'. This is not a dig at Facebook or Twitter. I think social media is an excellent and important form of communication and the technology behind it is mindboggling. However, time spent on these sites needs to be used wisely.

- **Don't be tempted to look at work-related social media sites during your free time.**
Almost all organisations use social media to promote their core business. You may convince yourself that it is useful in the evenings to see what your company and others say on such platforms (e.g. blogs, reports, etc.) just to 'keep up to date and see what the opposition are doing'. However, you need to ask yourself why you are doing this. Is it really necessary? By looking at these sites, you are clearly not relaxing your mind, and in fact you are still working. If you find something noteworthy, good or bad, it may act as a hidden

trigger mechanism and set a cascade of work-related thoughts in motion. Best not to go there in the first place. Ask yourself if it is really work you are doing, or are you doing this to pass the time in the evenings? If it was really important work, work with a capital 'W', this should be something you need to do during the day when you can give it your full attention. And if it is important you should be given time at work to pursue this activity.

- Outside working hours disable the automatic email forward function on your electronic devices.

  Many of us allow our work emails to be pushed to our personal phones. It is not 100 per cent clear why we do this, and we need to question our motives for doing so. Is it to keep up with the torrent of emails or to impress upon other people that we are busy and important? One reason I often hear for setting up this forwarding function is that an email can be quickly dealt with and this is easier in the long run, as it prevents a backlog building up. Although this can be useful during the working day, especially if you are away from your work station, it becomes counterproductive outside of work. A key principle of switching off is being proactive and taking control during your own leisure time. Unless specifically arranged in advance with your line manager (you may be 'on call' certain evenings during the week), we should feel free to turn off the phone. If it helps during the working day to have your emails pushed to your smartphone, this is fine; however, outside office hours, set your device only to automatically forward emails between certain hours, say, between 8 a.m. and 6 p.m. If necessary, activate an out-of-office reply saying you don't answer emails outside office hours.

- Don't check your phone within an hour of going to bed.

  Many of us take our phones to bed, for safety and security, and use them as alarm clocks. Try to avoid making calls, checking emails and texting at least thirty but preferably sixty minutes before going to bed, and never — unless absolutely necessary — use your phone in bed. The bright backlight given off by smartphones and tablets has been shown to cause melatonin suppression, which can disrupt sleep onset.

- Don't take the phone to bed.
  What is the first thing you do in the morning as soon as you switch off the alarm? Do you check the phone to see if anyone has emailed or texted? Some people tell me they check their smartphone/tablets even before they get out of bed. This cannot be a good start to the day. If you make it a habit to check your phone as soon as you wake up you will condition your mind to think about work as soon as you wake, so even if you wake up early to go to the bathroom during the night your mind will start generating work-related thoughts. If you kick-start your day by thinking about work issues your time before work is dominated by work. If you feel the need to check in before you leave for work, make this the last thing you do in the morning. If you can, wait until you have had breakfast and have got ready for work, and then switch on the phone.

- Leaving your contact details when you are on holiday.
  What are your rules for using smartphones and other electronic devices on holiday? Do you, as soon as you reach your hotel, ask the receptionist for the Wi-Fi password? Be honest with yourself. Would you miss such devices if you left them at home? A colleague of mine sent her line manager an email knowing full well he was on holiday in Turkey, and so wasn't expecting or anticipating a reply until he returned. However, to her amazement she got an answer within five minutes of hitting the send button. It was as if he was just sitting there waiting to answer emails — and he

probably was. How is this a holiday? A holiday should be time spent away from work. There are, however, some people who may need to be contactable during emergencies, and it is foolish to think everyone can simply switch their mobile off when on vacation. If you need to be contactable, why not leave the hotel details? It is normally all too easy today for someone to call you on your mobile. Make your own rules and negotiate with your partner/family or children.

- Unwind with a board game.

  If you enjoy playing games, another very good way to distract your mind from work-related thoughts is to play a board game. It may seem old-fashioned in the face of modern computer games and social media sites but board games can be enjoyed by people of all ages. There are many games on the market, so if Monopoly, Scrabble or Trivial Pursuit are not for you, I am sure you will find others. One of my favourite games is Rummikub, which is both engaging and fun for all ages. Why not choose one night every week or month when you have a technology-free evening and sit around the dining table and play games. Playing games is a great way to unwind after a busy day. Games are fun, distracting and a good way of socialising.

- Toilet texting.

  Finally, I can't leave this section without talking about toilet texting. Be honest, are you a toilet texter? A bathroom break used to serve a function — as a break — but not any more. You will be amazed how many people tell me (once I get to know them) they use their mobile devices in the loo — even at work — to do work-related tasks. I know it sounds gross but I suspect that the majority of readers have done this more than once. As far as I can tell, there are two camps here: some people think toilet texting is a waste of time, while others feel it aids productivity. In one recent survey half of those aged between eighteen and twenty-nine admitted using their phone on the loo. Toilet texting may be an evolutionally inevitability but to me it appears that the last bastion of privacy is now lost!

19
Vacations and mini breaks

'No man needs a vacation so much as the man who has just had one'

Elbert Hubbard

The above quote may seem true, but the truth is we all need to get away from the demands of life and take time out once in a while. We need a break from work, and a holiday gives us a chance to relax and recharge our batteries. Holidays enable us to spend some quality time with our partners, our children and our friends. It is remarkable how a change of scenery can make us feel refreshed and ready to face work once more. A holiday renews and fortifies our mental strength to tackle the demands of work. It is also a good way of spending time with people you don't spend regular time with. Studies have shown, not too unsurprisingly, that vacationers are happier than non-vacationers.

The magic is in the planning

The restorative properties of taking a break have long been recognised and appreciated. Research, however, tends to show that the effects of taking a holiday fade within a few days or weeks. Most studies show that stress and burnout decrease during and immediately following a vacation, but return to former levels within a month. This has led some people to think holidays are overrated. However, a holiday also gives us lasting memories, something to reflect on when things are not going too well. Also, holidays give us something to look forward to especially when the going gets tough. A lot of the magic surrounding a holiday comes from the planning and anticipation before you go away. I remember as a child looking forward to going away with my family, and what seemed like ages until it eventually came around, of dreaming what the place would be like, the activities we would do, etc. As adults when things at work are not going too well, and we are under a lot of stress, simply thinking about our holiday can cheer us up and see us through the day. Looking forward to a holiday can help us cope when stressors build. A study by a group of Dutch researchers found that there is also a psychological boost pre-holiday.[1] They compared happiness ratings in a sample of vacationers and non-vacationers and found that the former reported more happiness, especially just before going on holiday.

Academic studies have examined the effects of holidays on happiness and life satisfaction, and the general finding suggests that, post-vacation, life satisfaction is reduced. This may be taken by some to suggest that holidays are a waste of time and therefore best avoided. It is easy to jump to the wrong conclusion when simply looking objectively at the data. However, there may be more going on here. A holiday not only gives us a chance to spend time away from work, and experience new environments; holidays also give us time to reflect spiritually and see the bigger picture about life and work. Holidays give us a chance to clear our heads and think about the meaning of our work: 'Why am I working eighty hours a week in order to pay for my expensive house that I never have time to use?' Holidays give us a balanced view of the world, and people who take holidays are more satisfied with their life and their work. There is more to life than simply working.

Forty per cent of workers never take their full holiday entitlement

It may come as a surprise to many people but workers in the UK have the greatest holiday entitlement in the world. The top five countries with the best allowance are (in descending order) the United Kingdom, Poland, Austria, Bolivia and Denmark. In the ten top countries Bolivia is the only non-European one. The top five with the least statutory holiday entitlement are (in ascending order): the USA, the Philippines, Thailand, China and Canada. Historically, paid holidays are a very modern invention. The idea of having four paid weeks away from work would have seemed a wild dream at the beginning of the nineteenth century. This gradually changed over time. In the 1920s most workers in Britain were taking a week's paid leave, and this increased to two weeks by the 1950s. Often, however, a worker had to have been with their employer for a full twelve months in order to be entitled to a paid holiday. Unfortunately, some casual workers never stayed long enough in the same job to be entitled to a paid holiday.

Many health professionals, myself included, now believe that taking a regular holiday should not be considered an expensive luxury but as a necessity. A holiday should be considered a given; something that is part of our fabric of life. Moreover, I believe that taking time away from work should be compulsory. Amazingly, 40 per cent of workers do not take their full holiday allowance. One reason for this is that some people say they are simply too busy; another is that some workers are too worried about the threat of redundancy to take their full annual leave. It is thought that more than four million people fail to take advantage of their full holiday allowance, a number that included me until quite recently. Other reasons workers give for not taking their full quota is worrying that others may take credit for their work in their absence, being judged by colleagues for lacking commitment for daring to take time away during busy periods, or simply not planning leave and running out of time before the year ends. Some people feel that if they take time off, their work will simply pile up and they will therefore have more to do when they return. A typical comment is: 'There is nobody who can really do my job and cover me when I'm away, and everything just gets stacked up to greet me on my return.'

You probably have a list of all the places in the world you would like to see and experience. It may be visiting Cuba before it changes beyond all recognition. It could be taking your children to Florida so they can enjoy the magic of Disney World before they are too old. It may even be a long overdue skiing trip. It needn't be a luxury holiday. You may have always wanted to do voluntary work for a couple of weeks in Africa, or walk across the Andes. We all have dreams and I'm afraid they will only remain dreams unless you take the initiative and start planning. If you don't take your full holiday entitlement you might come to regret this as wasted opportunity. I suspect that few people say to themselves on their death bed, 'I wish I had taken fewer holidays and done more work'. Quite the reverse, I would imagine. People with older children will realise that time with family is important and can never be replaced. This is another reason why taking our holidays is important.

How about taking a mini vacation?

Another great way to recharge the batteries is to take a mini break. Mini breaks can be a great way to explore cities, whether you prefer walking around museums, looking at the architecture, or just sitting quietly in a café or bar and watching the world go by. For some people it may mean spending a weekend playing golf or relaxing in a spa, while for others it can be a retreat into solitude. As the saying goes, 'a change is as good as a rest'. Taking a couple of days or more off work can provide many benefits. Not only does it give us a chance to be away from the daily demands of work (reducing the temptation to check emails, etc.), therefore offering respite from work, but it also provides us with the opportunity to actively engage in potential recovery activities, and it gives us 'quality' time to spend with family and friends without the distraction of work. Mini breaks are very beneficial; not only do they force you to distance yourself physically from work, they can also give your brain a mental vacation. If you go to an interesting place you will psychologically detach from work. It is really a win-win situation, as a short break increases our wellbeing, mood and vigour and will give us an increase in work engagement once back at work. Thus, our employers can benefit from us taking a break!

If it is good enough for the President of the USA ...

Dwight D. 'Ike' Eisenhower, the thirty-fourth President of the USA, was renowned for taking many weekend vacations. He argued that he did so in order to maximise his creative ability.

Take action now and start planning your holidays

Taking paid leave from your employer is not a privilege but a statutory right. Good employers know that rested and recuperated workers function better and are more committed to their jobs. Thinking about it from the perspective of an employer for a moment, would you rather have a rested, fresh, enthusiastic worker brimming with ideas and raring to go? Or a fatigued and stale employee who only really wants to go home and sleep? This is a no-brainer.

What to do

Plan in advance: book your holidays as soon as you can at work. This will also give your employer time to plan for when you are away. In addition, plan some mini vacations in advance and choose the weekends when you would like to go away. Look for special offers. Some hotel chains have very good deals. You could use trip planning sites or phone up the hotel direct. You don't need to pay a fortune to stay in a quality hotel. Many good hotel chains have special offers and many include free evening meals or free meals for children. You needn't stay in a hotel if you are visiting family or friends.

Although it is nice to pamper yourself now and again, you don't need to stay in a top resort in order to unwind and get away from work. Weather permitting, you could go camping. There are many campsites that offer a relatively cheap but reasonable standard of comfort. Camping is also an excellent way to relax. You could also rent a cottage. Over the summer months these become expensive, unless you can get a cancellation, but during the winter many of these properties are difficult to rent out and the owners are only too pleased to let you have them at a discount.

Look at low-cost airline deals. Sometimes these come with rental cars and other perks. A Dutch friend of mine spent a long weekend in Scotland and got a flight, rental car and hotel for less than the price you would normally pay for theatre tickets in London for a family of four.

How to
approach work

Overview

In the previous part I discussed exercises and techniques you can practise to take control of your life outside of work in order to help you relax your mind during your leisure time. However, it is not just what you do out of work that can help you switch off; there is actually a lot you can change during your working day. We can structure our working day to make us more focused, and productive, and in doing so we make it easier for us to switch off and relax the mind once we leave work.

In Part III I demonstrate practical systems and exercises you can adopt during your working day to help in this process. I discuss time-management issues, dealing with interruptions, the importance of nurturing good social relationships at work, and why we should take regular breaks. Included in this part is a chapter discussing how we can use our commute more efficiently, too.

It has become more acceptable, and even encouraged in some organisations, to work from home at least one day per week. At home people are free from the everyday work distractions and so can concentrate on a specific piece of work. They also save time and possibly money by not commuting. However, for people who conduct their business from home there is no natural physical boundary to separate them from their work and therefore some home and self-employed workers find it difficult to escape from work at the end of the day. I am often asked if anything can be done. I have therefore included a chapter for people who regularly work from home. Even if you don't work from home during the working week, many people will do some work over the weekend, and therefore you may find that some of the principles of home working apply.

**20
Make
breaks
count**

'There is virtue in work and there is virtue in rest. Use both and overlook neither'

Alan Cohen

I think it is reasonable to assume in the twenty-first century that workers should be able to work in a safe and secure environment. We would find it unacceptable for our workers to injure themselves or die while in paid employment. In the same vein, I also think it is reasonable today to expect an employee to come home at the end of the day in a good state of mental and physical health. People who continually work under demanding conditions are at a high risk of becoming fatigued and burnt out. It is not acceptable for anybody to be so mentally and physically drained by work that they are unable to enjoy the few hours of leisure time before bed. Surely part of the reward of working is to have enough energy at the end of the day to devote time to hobbies, learning or to spend time with family or friends.

The great British tea break

Tea drinking in Britain dates back to at least the seventeenth century and even appears in the diaries of Samuel Pepys. On 25 September 1660, following an afternoon discussing foreign affairs with some fashionable and wealthy friends, Pepys wrote: 'and afterwards did send for a cupp of Tee (a China drink) of which I never drank before.'

The origin of the tea break is more difficult to trace, but the practice of stopping work during the morning has been going on for over 200 years. In those days, workers — particularly farm labourers — would start work at 5 or 6 a.m. and some employers started to serve food and free tea in the mornings. The afternoon tea break was also adopted by some employers. Over time, and particularly during the twentieth century, this would eventually develop into the modern tea break. Incredibly, but unfortunately true, between 1741 and 1820 some industrialists and landowners tried to ban the tea break as they thought that taking a break and drinking tea made their workers lazy and slothful. Thinking today couldn't be further from this: we now know that regular (tea) breaks play a vital part in the day to help maintain a positive attitude towards work. It is hard to conceive of a time before the tea break, so much is the notion of stopping for a cuppa a part of the fabric of British culture.

Quiet time is not wasted time

One way to counter the effects of strain is periodically to build in blocks of time when you are going to sit back, rest and recharge your batteries. There are other benefits to taking a break: people who are rested tend to be more creative, make better decisions and are generally more productive. It is good sometimes simply to sit back and unwind. We need to get out of the mindset of thinking that taking a break is a waste of time. It is not only wrong to think that stopping work and taking a break is wasted time and not important, it is also narrow-minded and stupid, and counterproductive. Sometimes we are simply too busy to see the wood for the trees.

The American motivational speaker and author Earl Nightingale once stated: 'If, instead of working on making more money, the average businessperson would spend an hour each and every day in quiet contemplation of how to be of greater and more creative service to his clientele, he and they would be the richer for it.'

Before you make an important decision, have a snack

Our attention span is not infinite. There is only a limited amount of time we can fully concentrate and attend to a task before our mind starts wandering. When our attention span begins to reach its limit, we are easily distracted. When this happens we are at our most vulnerable for making mistakes. Our ability to focus on a specific problem or issue varies, depending on our goal. Estimates vary as to the length of the average attention span, and there are wide individual variations; however, most people can sustain their attention for about forty minutes. There are a number of factors that affect attention and our ability to concentrate, and our attention will vary depending on how tired or hungry we are, the time of day and how much stress we are under. Did you know that defendants are statistically more likely to be let off or given a lighter sentence if their case is heard at certain times of the day? If you find yourself in front of a judge or magistrate, you would do better if your case was heard just after lunch or first thing in the morning following breakfast.

In an interesting study reported in the *Proceedings of the National Academy of Science of the USA* by academics from the Ben Gurion University of the Negev, Israel, and the Columbia Business School,

New York, researchers examined the percentage of favourable decisions by judges over a period of ten months. Judgments were pronounced over three distinct sessions: before a morning snack, between the morning snack and lunch and following lunch. In total 1,112 judicial rulings were examined by the researchers. Amazingly, they found that the likelihood of a favourable ruling was greater at the beginning of the working day, or after a food break. That is, the defendant was more likely to be given parole if the judge had just been on a break. The exact reason why judges appear more lenient after a break is not known and could be due to a number of reasons. However, as the authors speculated, it is most likely to be related to increased glucose levels. Glucose is the primary source of energy for our body cells. Glucose levels are usually at their lowest in the morning, typically before the first meal of the day, and rise up to two hours after a meal. Thus blood glucose levels are constantly changing throughout the day and they tend to be lower just before a meal. When we eat our blood glucose levels rise. We know that rest breaks are also good for replenishing mental resources and improving mood. Obviously these findings are important and need replicating; nonetheless, it is slightly worrying that someone's fate could be based on whether or not the judge had time for his or her customary cake and coffee in the morning. Studies have shown that employees who engage in relaxing activities during their lunch breaks also report less fatigue.

Some people believe that as a society our attention span is decreasing and they put this down to modern technology, especially television and the internet. Because of the way internet pages are set up, it encourages the browser to move quickly and effortlessly from one page to another. Hyperlinks are there to allow us to do this easily. It has been estimated that most users spend less than a minute browsing a webpage, and most people make a judgement of between ten and twenty seconds as to whether or not to stay on that page. It is possible to increase your attention span, but you need to train your mind and practise just as you would if you were trying to increase your cardiovascular fitness. Start small, say ten minutes at first. Set a timer if you need to and then focus on a task without being distracted. Gradually, over a period of time, increase the length of time just as you would increase your running intervals if preparing for a marathon. You also need to make sure you have breaks. Don't try going more than forty minutes without a break.

Take a walk and develop a theory

Not everyone can expect to come up with such ground-breaking theories but we all need time out to think and reflect. Charles Darwin (1809 – 1882), the great English naturalist and the author of *The Origin of Species* (1859), would habitually walk around the outer edge of his property five times every day at noon, often accompanied by his fox terrier Polly. His walk would take him along a small copse lined with hazel, alder, lime, hornbeam, birch, privet, dogwood and holly, encircled by a sandy path — hence the name the Sandwalk. For Darwin the Sandwalk was a place for contemplation, and meditation, and it is thought that many of his ideas, including his theory of evolution, came to him while walking around his 'thinking path'.

The Hungarian physicist and inventor Leó Szilárd is credited with conceiving a number of inventions that have changed mankind, including the idea of the electron microscope, the cyclotron linear accelerator and the nuclear chain reaction. In 1933, as the story goes, after reading an article in *The Times* about the report by Lord Rutherford (the Nobel Prize-winning New Zealand physicist and head of the Cavendish Laboratory in Cambridge) in which Rutherford described the process of splitting the atom by bombarding it with protons, Szilárd had disagreed with Rutherford's conclusion that it was not possible to harness the energy released. In fact, Rutherford suggested that anyone who believed it was possible to harness the source of the power by splitting the atom was 'talking moonshine'.

Szilárd dwelt almost obsessively on the problem but could not come up with a solution. Then, one grey, dismal morning in London, as he was waiting for the traffic lights to change near his hotel in Southampton Row, the answer came to him in a flash. He conceived the idea of a chain reaction, whereby a neutron fired at an atom would release two neutrons, each of which would hit another atom which in turn released two more neutrons, and so on, resulting in a massive release of energy.

Plan your breaks as well as your tasks

You don't have to be a brilliant thinker or a motivational speaker to benefit from taking time out during the day to reflect and ponder. However, it is very important to take time out and relax during the day. In order to do this you must plan your day and set up a daily routine. If you have your own office it may be a lot easier as you can close the door, step away from the desk and even do some stretching exercises if you wish. If you have tea- and coffee-making facilities close to hand, or within a relatively short walk, make yourself a cup. Even if you work in an open-plan office or work within a team, you should be able to find ways to have a break. If you find yourself getting stuck on a problem or feel your attention span wandering, get away from your work station for a while. Often the solution will just come to you, or perhaps a colleague you happen to bump into may provide you with the answer. Once you have had a break you will be more refreshed and ready to focus on the task in hand.

Take a break and recharge the batteries

While planning the day, make time for breaks. We find that people who have difficulty switching off from work tend also not to take breaks at work; or when they do take breaks they do not use the time restoratively. Like our attention span, our energy is not infinite, and we need to think of it in these terms. We only have so much energy or attention during the day. Think of energy as you would a petrol tank. A car engine requires petrol to work, and as we drive we burn petrol and the tank empties. In order to reach our destination on a long journey we have to periodically refill the tank.

Just as when we do heavy physical work, so we also need energy when we do mental work in order to think and reason effectively. During the day our energy tank is slowly running down and it needs refuelling by taking rests and topping up with water and calories. It is a good idea, therefore, not to use the same resources during your break as you would when working. For example, if your job involves working on a keyboard and looking at a computer screen for long hours, it is not a good idea to start surfing the web or shopping online during your break. Such activities are not restorative as they use the same or very similar resources to the one you have been using. By doing the same or very similar activities to work during your break you run the risk of overtaxing your biological system, and therefore increase your risk of developing strain and fatigue. You wouldn't expect to see a bricklayer during his break start working on a different part of the wall he had been working on.

Try a micro break or two

The importance of taking micro breaks was demonstrated in a study by Fritz and colleagues,[1] in the USA. In the study 214 employees working in professional and/or clerical positions, e.g. finance, human resources, general administration and sales, were asked to list the extent to which they engaged in a number of strategies in order to manage their energy levels at work.

The top five most common work-related strategies were:

(1) checking email,

(2) switching tasks,

(3) making a to-do list,

(4) offering help to a work colleague, and

(5) talking to a co-worker or supervisor.

Surprisingly, none of these activities were related either positively or negatively to self-reports of vitality or fatigue. The participants were also asked to rank the extent to which they engaged in micro-recovery break activities (short breaks) during the working day. The top five most common activities were: (1) drinking some water, (2) having a snack, (3) going to the bathroom, (4) drinking a caffeinated beverage, and (5) doing some form of physical activity, including walking or stretching. Of these top five strategies, only 'drinking a caffeinated beverage' was associated with less vitality. With regard to fatigue, a somewhat different pattern emerged. Fatigue was associated with 'having a snack', 'going to the bathroom', and 'drinking a caffeinated beverage'. Thus, these strategies were associated with, and presumably were utilised when, the workers were feeling particularly fatigued.

The question of real interest is which strategies are most related to vitality at work. In order of magnitude, they were: (1) learn something new, (2) focus on what gives me joy in my work, (3) set a new goal, (4) do something that will make a colleague happy, (5) make time to show gratitude to someone I work with, (6) seek feedback, (7) reflect on how I make a difference at work, and (8) reflect on the meaning of my work. Intriguingly, these strategies can be classified as relating to notions of learning, relationships and meaning at work. The only one work-related strategy that was negatively associated with vitality was 'vent about a problem'. Thus it seems that letting off steam to a colleague does not increase vitality, and in fact results in just the opposite effect.

We are all different in the amount of effort we can expend before we become tired and fatigued, and there are clearly individual differences in the time we need to feel rested and recovered. However, what is common to us all is that we need to sustain our energy levels. People may also pursue or modify their recovery strategies when they are already fatigued. When fatigued, people may drink more coffee for the caffeine buzz, but research has shown this is not a good habit as drinking too much caffeine can interfere with sleep, therefore leading to further fatigue. In general, longer or more frequent rest breaks have been shown to be most beneficial to health, and longer, more frequent rest breaks have been associated with fewer stress symptoms and fewer job-related accidents and injuries. Repeated ten-minute breaks that involve some gentle physical activity have also been shown to result in decreased fatigue and increased mood.

Your computer mouse carries three times more germs than the average toilet seat

One final word of caution: it is also not very hygienic to eat your lunch at your desk, especially as bits of food fall on to your keyboard. One study found that workstations are breeding grounds for harmful bacteria and germs. The average computer mouse carries three times more harmful bacteria than a toilet seat! Apparently, male office workers are the worst culprits, as their mouses contain 40 per cent more bacteria than their female counterparts. It is common now for people to eat at their desks, and some will continue typing while they are eating, or finish eating and carry on working without washing their hands. So not only is it not good to stay in the same place too long, but the bacteria on desk surfaces and computer accessories can pose a risk to health.

If possible, get away from your desk. There are many benefits and few drawbacks to eating lunch away from the desk. Get into the habit of getting away from your workstation, if only for half an hour. Stand up, take a walk outside, or walk around the office if you can't get out. If there is a park nearby go and have a walk or find a nice quiet bench to sit on and enjoy your lunch. If you do this, you will find that you will have a clearer head, you will be more productive and less fatigued in the afternoon.

21
Your
unwinding
ritual

'It's a hard thing to leave any deeply
routine life, even if you hate it'

John Steinbeck

Fifty per cent of workers spend ninety minutes per day or more commuting to work!

In an ideal world we could divide our twenty-four-hour working day into three equal chunks of time: eight hours working, eight hours on leisure activities and eight hours sleeping. If only life was that organised and segmented. Typically, most of us spend a good portion of our 'free' time getting to and travelling home from work. A study published in 2013 showed that the average UK worker spends forty-one minutes commuting to work every day. This is the average, but it doesn't really reflect what is going on at the extremes. This study also showed that a staggering 1.84 million Brits spend three hours or more getting to or travelling home from work. Over the week these so-called 'super-commuters' spend what amounts to a whole day travelling.

Interestingly, the number of individuals spending ninety minutes or more commuting to work has soared by over 50 per cent over the last five years. Apparently accountants have the longest daily commute, at 75.6 minutes, followed by IT workers, at 65.6 minutes. IT workers on average travel 38.5 miles, while fitness club employees have the shortest travelling distance of 12.6 miles and this may be a reflection of the working hours they keep, with early mornings and late finishes being the norm in the leisure industry.

Today most people tend to commute to and from work. I will discuss how to unwind from work if you work from home in chapter 25. For most people the commute is an inevitable part of their day, and can be quite stressful at times. There are often traffic jams and trains and buses tend to be overcrowded and sometimes late in the rush hour. When I ask people when they start to unwind, most will say not until they get indoors. In this chapter I would like you to take a different approach, and start thinking about unwinding not only on the commute home but also while you are still working. This may seem counterintuitive and you may feel that you will get less done, but research tells us that people who use their free time to mentally detach from work are more likely to be engaged and productive at work. If you commute to your place of work there is a natural boundary between your home and working environment. Think about the two environments for a moment. Your work is where you work, and your home is your place of leisure. Your working life is normally controlled by external forces (e.g. deadlines, etc.), and in theory you have a higher degree of control at home (although we all have certain commitments). However, if you don't psychologically disengage from work, it is as if you didn't leave your place of work and you are in fact still working. You need to condition yourself to start the unwinding process by developing an unwinding routine or ritual that you can easily follow. You need to create a psychological boundary between your workstation and your home life.

Develop an unwinding ritual

Before I discuss the unwinding ritual in detail, I would like you first to think about your commute home, starting from just before you leave the office or your place of work. Write down all the steps you take in getting home. What do you do? Is it a gentle transition from the office to your car, train, bus or bike/cycle? If you cycle do you have to negotiate the traffic? If you catch the train or bus do you rush to the bus or railway station? If you drive, how does the drive home make you feel? While you are driving is your mind still occupied with work thoughts, the meetings you had that day and the extra work you now have to do as the result of the meeting? Maybe you said something at work which you now regret and you keep thinking about it. Or do you swear and get frustrated by the traffic congestion?

There are many behaviours we can engage in to help us unwind. However, we need to engage in certain behaviours and develop a routine to signal to our brains that the working day is over. It is now my time. I am not being paid any more, so it is my time to relax. In this exercise I would like you to start planning your own unwinding ritual, something you can do on a regular basis. I have suggested a 'leaving the office ritual' below, but it is important that you develop your own ritual, something that will work for you. It may be easier to develop three rituals: a leaving the office ritual, the commute home ritual and what to do when you get home ritual. Once you develop these you can put them all together. However, simply having an unwind ritual is one thing; the next step is to put it in place and practise it. The more you do this, the more easily it will develop into a habit, and, as we know, habits are difficult to break. By doing this, you will condition your brain to unwind at the end of the working day. If you start doing routines just before you leave work, this will start to signal to the body and brain that it is time to start unwinding (*'This is now my time'*).

Start to unwind before you leave work

The end of day ritual

When do I start my unwinding ritual? You can start this while you are still at work. Towards the end of the day do something in particular that signals to the brain that the working day is coming to an end. You could start by tidying your desk if you work in an office or putting your tools away if doing manual work. Some people make a list of the jobs that need doing the following day but I personally don't find this useful. I have an ongoing list that is continually changing, so I add jobs to the list throughout my day. You may have a cup or mug that needs washing. You may also tackle one type of task towards the end of the day, such as writing references or backing up files, etc. This is an example of an unwinding ritual.

> *Tidy papers away from desk; shred anything important, and put in the recycling bin. Switch off the laptop and release from the docking station, place in filing cabinet and lock the drawer. Wash and dry mug and tidy away in the desk drawer. Check the heater is unplugged, check windows are closed and plants don't need watering. Switch off light and close and lock the office door.*

This is my simple unwinding routine.

At the end of the working day some people find it beneficial to put everything away so their workstation is neat and tidy ready for the next day. It is strange but clearing the desk or workstation can also help to clear the mind.

The commute home ritual

For many people the commute home is seen as a means to an end — they just want to get home as fast as possible — and in some respects this is true for most of us. And, let's face it, when you have had a hard day at work it is only natural to want to go home as quickly as possible and put our feet up. On one level, this is perfectly acceptable, but I also think we are missing an opportunity. Let's think for a moment about the way people approach their journey home. Often you see people rush out of the office, hurry to their cars or rush to a train or bus. Inevitably, the bus is late and then they start to moan, get agitated and stressed. Once the bus arrives, typically two at a time, there is then the fight for a seat. This also applies to the train, as people rush along the platform to find a seat. If people drive to work, driving home between 5 and 6.30 p.m. is normally the worst time to be on the roads. It's not called the rush hour for nothing, although, ironically, anyone who drives in cities seldom moves that quickly. A survey of rush-hour speeds in May 2013 found Jamaica Road in Southwark, south London, to have an average rush-hour speed between 8 and 9 a.m. of only 0.08 miles an hour. It was calculated that the average pedestrian normally walks about forty times faster! It is amazing and worrying — not least because of the impact on the environment — how many productive hours are wasted trying to get to and from work.

On arriving home people are just as stressed as when they were at work. Instead of arriving home refreshed and recuperated, the commute has added to your daily stress levels. Not only are you fatigued as the result of working hard all day, you also add to your fatigue and to your frustration with the drive home. The commute home, if not done right, can further deplete your energy and increase your stress levels. People who get stressed by their drive home are still mentally and physiologically aroused when they get indoors, and they naturally start thinking about the bad day at work as well as the drive home. You then have to start unwinding not only from work but also from the drive home. People vary as to the length of time it takes them to mentally unwind once they arrive home. For some it takes a matter of minutes, but others may need to be left alone for half an hour before they even start interacting with their partner or family. They sit down, maybe grab a coffee, beer or glass of wine and try to unwind by being by themselves for a while.

One person I spoke to said he found it particularly difficult to adjust from work to home. He worked in a fast-paced, highly stressful and pressured environment, making financially important decisions. On returning home each evening, he found it difficult to adjust to the change in pace in being with his family. He explained this well with a driving analogy. When he got home his brain was still working overtime and racing; he said it was like driving on the motorway at ninety miles an hour and then suddenly having to drop his speed to ten miles an hour, as if approaching a school. His mind was still racing at full speed but his children just wanted him to be their dad; someone to read them a story, to watch a cartoon or do some colouring with, or just have fun with. But he found it extremely hard to reduce his speed and adjust to a slower speed. Instead of using the change of environment as a distraction, his brain was still too focused on work. During our meetings we worked on the notion of using the last hour of the day to start to unwind, so that he did not leave the office and arrive home at Mach speed.

Make your commute home work for you

Why not use the commute home as time to adjust, as a transition from work to home? Don't think of the commute as an inconvenience — you have to do it anyway — so why make yourself stressed? There are a number of ways you can use the commute in your favour. One of my friends works in London and, to avoid the rush, he gets to work really early in the morning so that he can leave at 4 p.m. to miss the rush hour. Rather than take the Tube, which can be quite stuffy at times, he catches the bus, which is quite empty and quiet at this time. His journey takes him probably a couple of minutes longer by bus but usually no more, but he likes the journey and likes looking out of the window to unwind, especially on the way home.

If you have a job that allows you to work flexible hours or you have a certain period within which you have to be at work, why not try this approach? It will need a bit of planning before you find the solution that works for you but it will be well worth it. By arriving early and leaving at 4 p.m., my friend also finds he can get a lot done before anyone else arrives because he can focus uninterrupted on his work. He also finds that people will not expect anything more from him at the end of the day, as they know he has already put in a full day's work. What he has done is effectively trained his colleagues. This is obviously a win-win situation as both he and his employer benefit. On the rare occasions when there is a very important deadline, he will nonetheless stay later to complete the work.

If you use public transport to commute to work you can also use the travel time wisely. In the mornings you can start working on your way to work by not doing anything too taxing and you can gently kick-start your brain for the demands of the day. Think of it as an athlete warming up before an event. When you arrive at work, you can hit the ground running. However, on the way home, use the commute to unwind. Try to avoid checking emails or answering the phone. If you have a smartphone or laptop, why not use the technology in a positive way? Phone friends and family, listen to your favourite music, or watch a film on your laptop. You could also play games such as solitaire, Scrabble, or chess, or whatever the latest craze is. Some people prefer reading using a tablet or PC. It does not really matter what game we play or what we listen to in order to facilitate the unwinding process, so long as it helps us unwind on the commute home.

If you are one of these 'super-commuters' mentioned earlier, it is not a good idea to play games all the way home as this may be an unproductive use of your time. If you commute for an hour or more, try to leave work early but use the first forty minutes or so to complete work-related tasks, and then dedicate the remainder of the time to unwinding. Whatever you have been doing while you have been working I advise you to task-switch; that is, to switch to a task that requires different resources. For example, if you have been staring at a laptop screen for a long time, try to listen to some music or look out of the window; don't play a game that requires you to look at the screen or watch a film. Find a task that uses a different resource.

If your drive home takes you near a wood or scenic picnic area, why don't you try stopping there? If possible, stop and take a little time to walk, relax and ponder. You can use some of the mindfulness techniques I discussed in chapter 17. For example, be open to your senses and absorb your surroundings. Listen to the sounds of the birds, the trees rustling in the wind, twigs breaking underfoot, the ripple of a stream, etc. Pay attention to the smells, the fresh air entering and exiting your nostrils, the scent of the flowers. Feel the warmth or coldness against your skin. It is your choice whether you do this every night or just on one day per week. In urban environments, you could try to find a park to sit in to ponder and reflect on life, or even a café, bar or library. It doesn't really matter; it is for you to find a place where you can start to unwind. It may not be possible to do this every night, especially in the winter, but try to do it once or twice a week to see if it helps.

As soon as you get home ritual

What do you do as soon as you get home? Do you rush upstairs and get changed, have a shower or take a long bath? Do you immediately have dinner or do you wait a while? If you have a partner or children do you sit down and have a chat about your day or interact with your kids? If it is sunny, perhaps you go out into the garden. Maybe the first thing you do on getting indoors is to log on and check your emails to see if anything has come in since you left the office.

Similar to your leaving the office and your commute home ritual, you need to develop an 'as soon as I get home' ritual. Don't be tempted to check your emails. If you start responding this creates the wrong impression on a number of levels. It will give the impression that you are not in control and you don't really respect your own free time or family. Once you start responding to emails outside your working hours, this will set a precedent that is difficult to stop as people will begin to expect a response from you. Remember, you need to train your colleagues not to expect you to be available 24/7. You have a life that includes a job, not a job that is your life. Let others know that you care about both but don't let one take over the other. It is up to you which night of the week you start your unwinding experiment; however, I suggest you plan your unwinding routine over a weekend or at least a couple of days before you put it into action.

If you have a partner or children you may have to modify your home routine to suit different days and other people. Your partner may need picking up one evening, or to have the car, or your child may have an after-school routine. You need to build this into the ritual. For example, if your child needs picking up at a certain time why not arrive twenty minutes early and have a tea or coffee by yourself and read the paper. You can use this time to reflect on your working day if you wish. Whatever you decide to do, you must do it in a relaxing manner. Don't use the extra twenty minutes or so to write a report: you will run out of time and get frustrated. If you know you are going to have a few spare minutes to yourself at the end of a very busy day, you may find that you work more efficiently during the day, as you use the twenty minutes by yourself as a reward.

Some people I have spoken to prefer to be left alone for a few minutes when they get home. Of course, you need the buy-in and approval from your family before you engage in this behaviour as they may think you are being selfish, especially if your partner has been looking after the children all day and needs a break as much as you do. However, if you can find ten to fifteen minutes just to unwind, maybe sitting down with a cup of tea or coffee, in your favourite room or in a nice spot in the garden (weather permitting), just to let the working day pass, this will be most beneficial. You could include your partner if he or she is at home and spend a few minutes together chatting about the day. This is more difficult if you are both working and you arrive home at different times. Of course, it is a matter of negotiation and compromise, and you need to discuss your unwinding ritual with your partner or siblings. Importantly, put away everything that reminds you of work. Leaving your briefcase in the lounge or the work laptop on show will only serve to trigger work-related thoughts. I have even known (and I do this, too) people who wear reading glasses who have one pair for work and another for leisure. This sounds extreme but it does work. If you prefer you can take a shower, or simply change out of your work clothes into something more comfortable. Once your ten to fifteen minutes are up, you can enjoy the rest of your evening, and then you are ready to discuss the issues of the day in a more attentive way. There is nothing worse than having a hard day at work and then being hit with demanding questions or being confronted with the terrors of the day by your partner as soon as you come through the front door, especially when all you want to do is unwind and relax. This is the wrong time to start talking about important issues and the wrong time to vent your emotions. These things are best tackled later on during the evening, when you are both relaxed and you can discuss issues in a more logical, detached manner. If you occasionally have to work in the evening, once you have followed your unwinding ritual you will find that you are able to work more efficiently, and that you are less distracted than you used to be. Of course, I wouldn't advise you to make a habit of working during the evening.

If you have very young children much of what I say above may not be possible, but children themselves can prove to be a good source of distraction. If you do have young children you need to negotiate with your partner and work out a strategy that works for both of you. Children, especially young ones, require a lot of attention, and contrary to what you may think are very helpful in the unwinding process.

Be prepared to try different rituals and be prepared to change these slightly over time, especially during the winter and summer months. If you have a garden you could use that to help you switch off. We interviewed an individual who said that during the summer he always cuts the lawn when he gets home on Friday evenings. He said this was part of his unwinding ritual to signal to himself that the weekend had arrived. He enjoyed his garden and it played a big part in his unwinding routine. He would make sure he cut the lawn to relax and, by doing this, cutting the lawn on Friday evenings became part of his unwinding ritual during the summer months. If you do not have a garden or gardening is not your thing, this does not matter; the important issue is to find and develop your own unwinding ritual.

When do you start to mentally unwind from work?

Most people start to mentally prepare themselves to unwind as the weekend approaches. Our minds seem to unconsciously prepare us to do this. When we examine how workers unwind over the course of the working week we consistently find that people think about work more, and find it more difficult to switch off from work-related thoughts at the beginning of the week compared to the rest of the week. Monday to Thursday evenings are the days when people find it most difficult to unwind and switch off from work during their leisure. See the figure below. On Friday evenings people start to wind down naturally and we find the lowest work-related thoughts are reported on Saturday evenings, although there are many people who still think about work much of the time over the weekend. By Sunday evening most of us are starting thinking about work again. Workers often say that Sunday night is their worst night for sleep.

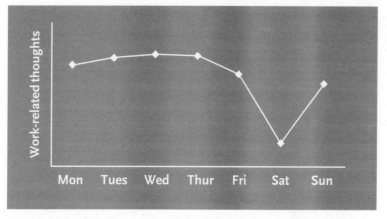

Figure 1. Thoughts about work issues during the evening across the week. This pattern is consistent across the UK and in other European countries in workers who work a five-day week.

You may notice yourself that some days you are better able to unwind than others. Make a note of what you do on these days/evenings and see if you can incorporate whatever you do to help you unwind on other evenings. Once you develop a successful unwinding process that you habitually follow, you will be amazed how refreshed you feel each morning, and how much more engaged and energised you are at work. The more times you practise your ritual, the sooner it will develop into a habit and you will find that you begin to unwind naturally during your leisure time.

22
Interruptions and unfinished tasks

'And I was having too much fun to stop now'

Jeff Lindsay

Have you ever watched a soap opera or a mini series on television and noticed that it invariably ends in a cliffhanger just before the music begins and the credits start to roll? Are they about to kiss? Will the husband come home and discover them? Will the person survive? Nearly all programme makers do this and there is a good reason why. Something uncompleted tends to play on the mind and is easily remembered; whereas something that is completed doesn't play on the mind so much, and completed tasks are easily forgotten.

An unfinished task plays on the mind

Have you heard of the Zeigarnik effect? In psychology, this refers to the phenomenon whereby people remember uncompleted or interrupted tasks better than completed tasks. Bluma Zeigarnik was a Russian psychologist who studied under Professor Kurt Lewin. Lewin noticed while in a restaurant that the waiter could remember what was on the unpaid bills but soon forgot the details of those that had been paid. In a series of experiments Zeigarnik aimed to replicate and explain the findings under laboratory conditions. In one set of studies she asked subjects to complete a series of small problems or tasks; for example, they had to put together a cardboard box. She stopped half of them as they were completing the tasks, while the other half were allowed to finish without interruption. Thus some people finished the tasks while others did not. Interestingly, when they were later asked to recall and name the different types of tasks/problems, the groups who were able to complete the tasks recalled fewer tasks, compared to the group who were interrupted while they were trying to complete them. In fact non-completers (interrupted during task completion) recalled 90 per cent more tasks compared to the completers. There are various explanations for this effect, and it may be related to tension reduction, as perhaps it could be advantageous in evolutionary terms if we are better able to remember something that is not completed. Interestingly, we find a similar related effect operating in people who find it difficult to switch off and unwind post-work. We find that people tend to ruminate about unfinished tasks but not over completed ones. For example, even though some people may not physically take work home with them they nevertheless think about their work during their free time, especially if it is an unfinished project.
Sarah said:

'I take work home mentally with me, and perhaps if there's something that's not been concluded or I've not heard from somebody that I was hoping to hear from, or you know, things like that, I will take that home, but not in respect of actually being able to do anything with it.'

How do you stop?

There are a couple of key strategies you can use to reduce the chances of being affected by having unfinished tasks at work. The first step, however, is to identify possible reasons. To this end, take a few minutes to reflect and write down why you have unfinished tasks in your working life. Is it because you have poor time-management techniques? Do you find it difficult to say no and take on too much work? Are you simply given too much work to do, or are you frequently distracted or interrupted when trying to complete your work?

My goals are always changing so I never complete them

I know what you are thinking because I hear it said quite often. People say, 'My work is constantly changing and when I finish one project another one starts'. Or, 'I have eight or more projects on the go at any one time so how can I possibly complete them all?' I agree, but so do a lot of people who don't have difficulty unwinding during the evening. It is almost inevitable that some projects do not get completed and tasks will remain unfinished at the end of the working day or week. If you are the type of person who is affected by this you need to take action.

First, you need to change your mindset about trying to complete everything at once. Next, break down the project or projects into bite-size tasks. Aim to complete a specific amount of work for any given task before you leave at night. If you don't complete it, examine why not towards the end of the day and readjust your goals for the following day. Finally, try not to take on large tasks towards the end of the week if possible. People who find it difficult to unwind are particularly prone to worry and ruminate about unfinished tasks once work-related thoughts are triggered. As you complete a task tick it off your list and secretly congratulate yourself on a job well done. It will then be off your mind.

Deal with interruptions

Unfinished tasks can be caused by a number of factors: having too much work to do in the time available, poor planning and organisational skills and a lack of training or ability. An unfinished task does not necessarily mean an unfinished project. It could also be an unresolved conflict or argument at work. It is good to work in a friendly environment with good work colleagues, and it is nice now and again for a colleague to drop by for a coffee or phone for a chat. However, being continually interrupted eats away at our time, and continually being interrupted can lead to feelings of irritation and tension, all of which add to our stress levels. Sometimes people interrupt you because they need a piece of information, and it may be easier to ask you than to find out themselves. So you end up helping someone complete their task at the expense of yours. In our research we find that some people don't mind being interrupted but many do, and being interrupted and not getting your work done makes it more difficult for people to unwind and relax as the unfinished project plays on their mind.

Remember that your time is precious. Some time-management books suggest we should treat time as a commodity or as a currency, but I disagree. With currency you can always try to get more, but once time has gone it has gone for ever. You cannot push back time. If a colleague wants to talk to you, let them do so when it suits you. It is your time they are stealing and they are stopping you completing your tasks, so don't let the time thieves take control.

You need to be honest with yourself about whether you like being interrupted or not. If you don't, there are many strategies you can use to reduce the likelihood of losing time because of interruptions. You may need to become more assertive, without being aggressive, saying, for example, 'I can do this but not at the moment as I have promised Joe I will finish this off by 5 p.m. today.' See the box below for useful techniques on dealing with interruptions.

Techniques for dealing with interruptions

Office environment

Leave bags or papers on the chair to stop people sitting down

Introduce a policy of red and green time. Green allows you to be interrupted, but red means not to be disturbed

Switch off email, mobile phones and Skype, etc., and disconnect your desk phone when you need to work intensively

Your posture

Don't make eye contact with the person. Focus on your computer screen or whatever you are doing

Keep a pen or pencil in your hand to indicate you are busy

Stand up and leave your office

Tell the person you are busy (be polite and say you will catch up once you have finished the project/task you are working on)

Don't be afraid to set limits. I have five minutes but really need to get this done (but I'd love to have a coffee and catch up)

Make a mental note of who is interrupting you. You may find one person is taking up more time than most.

23
Planning your day

'A goal without a plan is just a wish'

Antoine de Saint-Exupéry

As stated in the previous chapter, time is the one thing in life that we can't buy. We can buy fancy clothes, watches, cars and houses, but we can't buy back time. Once it has gone, it has gone for ever. If you miss your children growing up, their first day at school, their first school play, you will never have another chance to relive that experience. We all manage our time in different ways and most of us would think we are pretty good at time management, but I am sure if we analysed our day in detail most of us would see room for improvement. I don't want to be completely obsessed about time; however, most of us can manage our time better. I am not going to go into too much detail about time management (there are books devoted to the subject), but below I offer some techniques most people find useful.

I have read many books on time management and they all offer ways of increasing our productivity. However, one of the problems is that once we become more efficient it is easy to fall into the trap and take on more work. Before you know it you are back where you began, although now you feel completely trapped. The art is to get the appropriate amount of work completed on time and then say no to other requests, and fill your spare time with the things you want to do. Freeing up your time so you can concentrate on the things that give you personal satisfaction will make you more productive in return.

The first step is to look at our time use. Look at the box below. You can expand and copy this on to a piece of paper if you wish. In the left-hand column write down how you normally spend your time at work. Then, in the right-hand column write down what you would ideally like to spend most of your time doing. Think how you spend your time and what tasks really matter for you and your organisation. The next step (in the second box) is to work out how you can spend more time on the things you want to do, the things that push the organisation forward. Because of space limitations I have only left five rows but you may find you need more.

Complete the table below by noting how you currently spend your time and what you would ideally spend your time doing.

Actual time use	Ideal time use
Example: sitting in meetings I don't really need to be in	Working on creative projects that push the company forward
Example: spending too much time reading emails	Training staff
Example: spending time on low-value tasks – those tasks that don't add value to you or the organisation	

In the table below copy the items in from your actual time-use column and then decide what measures/procedures you can put in to place to free your time, so you can spend your time on the tasks that are important.

Actual time use	How to improve my use of time
Example: sitting in meetings I don't really need to be in	Only attend meetings I really need to attend
Example: spending too much time reading emails	Set a policy within the organisation requesting that people should not be mindlessly copied into emails when not absolutely necessary
Example: spending time on low-value tasks – those tasks that don't add value to you or the organisation	Identify those tasks that you can easily drop, delegate, etc.

Another good habit to adopt is to plan your day. This sounds straightforward but it's surprising how many people do not follow a clear plan during the day. Making lists is a very good strategy to follow and it's rewarding to cross off jobs once they are completed. However, allow sufficient time for each job on the list. Sometimes if the project is large it's not possible to complete it within one day or even a week so therefore you need to break it down into bite-size chunks. Don't expect to complete everything in one day. Breaking each job down into small, manageable tasks is psychologically beneficial as it gives us a sense of achievement once we cross them off the list. We don't usually think or ruminate about tasks that we have finished and therefore we don't think about them after work. Remember, while planning the day, make time for breaks.

Deception of the mind

I reported earlier that one of the reasons why people can't seem to escape from work is because they are nearly always working. They spend most of their available leisure time either physically doing work, as in writing reports, answering emails or dealing with correspondence, or mentally, by thinking about work or work issues. Another group of people I have encountered are those who are so preoccupied by work they continue to think or worry about work-related issues when not at work, but they do little to confront the issue. Interestingly, in some studies we find that those who say they can't escape from work-related thoughts, and complain of tension, tiredness and fatigue, actually work fewer hours (and are less productive) than people who can switch off during their leisure time. There may be many reasons for this but one reason they believe they work long hours is that continually thinking about work, and ruminating about what needs to be done, tricks the mind into thinking that you have done more work then you actually have. When we look more deeply into actual working patterns we also find some people who can't switch off are less productive because their mind keeps wandering and they do not concentrate on one specific task. Sometimes it may be better — as long as it doesn't become a habit — to stay an hour later to finish that piece of work, just to get it out of our heads.

Take action

Use action to cure fear and stop ruminating. Fear is one driver behind rumination. Waiting, as in inaction, makes people nervous and worry. It is often said that the minutes before going on stage are the most fearful and petrifying for most performers. While they wait to go on stage, actors start to worry about making mistakes, forgetting lines, while dancers may worry about falling over or forgetting a routine. Once on stage, once they take action, this fear immediately disappears. In most of our work we don't have to perform, unless we are making a presentation. It is always worse to be the last speaker in a conference symposium than the first. To combat the fear stop ruminating and take action. Don't put off making that phone call; don't wait until the perfect report comes to mind. Start writing, start taking action. Action — if it is the right form of action — feeds and builds confidence and combats fear. Inaction feeds and builds fear.

Work on one task at a time
Don't leave a simple task when it can be completed quickly. Set a specific amount of time each day or week to deal with those small but important issues. Once completed, they are off your list and your mind, leaving your head space to concentrate on other issues. Have

you ever thought, while watching TV or having dinner, 'I must make that phone call tomorrow', 'I must do such and such', and once such a thought comes to mind it then sets the mind off on one of its journeys?

Multi-tasking

We have only a limited working memory capacity and attention span. There is only so much we can pay attention to and, contrary to what we are sometimes told, there are not that many people who can truly multi-task. Multi-tasking is really rapid attention switching. This is draining, stressful and actually extremely unproductive. Women are reported to be better able to multi-task than men. However, it is well documented that women are more likely to suffer from tension headaches than men. And it has been said (although this may not apply to everyone) that this is due to continually switching attention from one task to another. This activity requires a lot of psychic energy.

The Monday morning team meeting

If possible, try to avoid team planning meetings on Monday mornings. Many companies adopt this strategy, reviewing what they did the previous week to see what projects did or didn't get finished. The downside to this is that people will start thinking about the Monday morning meeting on Sunday and in particular Sunday evening.Consequently many people do not sleep well on Sunday nights. Studies that have examined sleep and fatigue over the working week and weekend consistently show that the poorest quality of sleep and the highest levels of fatigue are actually reported immediately following the weekend. These findings oppose the notion that the weekend is good for recovery. In addition, a growing body of literature suggests that, following the weekend, there is actually a significantly increased risk of workers experiencing a range of psychological health problems including depression, suicide and physical issues, more specifically an increased risk associated with diseases of the cardiovascular system, including high blood pressure, stroke and heart attacks. One theory is that people who are at risk on Monday mornings are those who do not sufficiently relax and recover over the weekend.

Slow down. Realise that it's not about how fast you can be, it's about the outcome you achieve. Efficiency seems to be inversely related to speed, or, to put it the other way around, speed is inversely related to efficiency. Unless you are doing piecework, and getting paid the more you produce, if you work the result is that you will be given more work to do.

24
Friends
and colleagues

'Years and years of happiness only make us
realize how lucky we are to have friends that
have shared and made that happiness a reality'

Robert E. Frederick

In what has become a seminal study, Lisa Berkman and Leonard Syme[1] examined the association between social relationships and mortality over a nine-year period in people in Alameda County, California. They examined the network of friends of a large sample of some 6,928 individuals and divided them into three groups: those with a strong network of friends (people with high social support); those with a poor network of friends (people with low social support); and those in between. At the nine-year follow-up, they found that people who reported fewer social connections at the start of the study were more likely to have died over the intervening nine years. The most isolated people were at the greater risk of mortality. In fact, men were 2.3 times and women 2.8 times more likely to die if they were socially isolated (age-adjusted). Maybe those who were ill had fewer social ties in the first place, and so the findings are not that clear; however, the research also showed that the association between social contacts and mortality was independent of self-reported physical health status at baseline.

Socialising is an inherent human trait. Some creatures are solitary animals but humans, for one reason or another, have developed into social animals. There are obvious exceptions, but most people like to spend time with others. We do this via the family, through work and leisure activities. Companionship is a human trait.

There is a lot to be said for the above quote by Robert Frederick. Human intimacy is an antidote to stress. We know from the psychological literature that close, trusting friendships can not only help us to deal with stress, but they can also prevent stress from occurring. How can this work? If you have a problem at work a friend can help you deal with the emotional side of the issue. A good friend or colleague could calm us down, tell us to stop being so sensitive, or just agree with us that there is an issue and that it is now time to deal with it. Our friends can also help us physically with a problem. We may need help with something or maybe we need to borrow some equipment. A friend could lend us some money if necessary. If we become angry or upset about something that was said at work, and we begin to let it affect us and we dwell on the problem, a friend can get us out of this way of thinking before it spirals out of control. Hopefully a good friend can make us see sense before we do something rash and that we later regret. These little acts of friendship help us to deal with the effects of stress and by doing this it stops the stressor from taking a hold of our life.

It goes without saying that it feels better to work in a place in which there is a positive social atmosphere. Research has shown that positive relationships at work foster coherence and productivity. It is good for people to pull in the same direction. People feel more energised both physically and emotionally in a positive working culture. Positive relationships at work are associated with better cardiovascular health and greater immune functioning. For example, in one study a team of Finnish researchers[2] asked people from a range of occupations to wear heart-rate monitors over a twenty-four-hour working day. They divided the workers into three groups, those reporting high, medium and low social support at work. Social support at work was assessed via questionnaires with questions such as 'Do I have good relationships with my work colleagues?'. During the working day workers reporting the highest levels of social support at work had the lowest heart rate during work compared to those reporting medium and low social support at work. Interestingly, those reporting the highest social support at work — those who reported working with good colleagues and supervisors — also had the lowest heart rate during sleep. Thus, the effects of working in a cohesive and friendly environment at work spilled over into leisure time.

Intriguingly, in the study of employee of the year, discussed in chapter 11, the top employees emphasised the importance of working with good colleagues and having good relationships in their workplace. A good atmosphere at work was not just seen with immediate colleagues but also vertically throughout the organisation. Employees of the year actually stated that conflicts at work were a major obstacle. In terms of unwinding from work, we have also found (in a number of studies) that having good colleagues promotes the recovery process. Simply put, people who work with supporting colleagues ruminate less and unwind more quickly from work. Not unsurprisingly, however, the opposite is also true: a poor atmosphere at work, where they are back-stabbing and unsupportive colleagues, hinders the recovery process. For example, teaching, as we discussed earlier, is a very stressful occupation, and teachers always score high on stress measures. In a recent study of stress in schoolteachers we examined what factors at work influence a lack of unwinding after work. We expected student misbehaviour to be the key driver, as dealing with unruly children cannot be that easy, and thinking about unruly children must surely play on the mind. And, sure enough, when we examined different forms of stressors within the school, which included professional recognition needs, student misbehaviour, and colleagues, student misbehaviour was a factor, but it was not the key factor. The main factor, controlling all other factors, was work colleagues; that is, those who reported working with difficult unsupportive colleagues found it very difficult to mentally unwind after work. Thus, the key predictor in the unwinding process was support from colleagues.

Other research suggests that a working environment which is supportive and where there is a sense of cohesiveness helps workers to foster sustained energy levels and people tend to work more effectively. Workers are more engaged and report more vigour at work where there is good interaction between staff and supervisors.

Over the years we have conducted a number of studies examining how people mentally unwind from work, and one key aspect that appears to affect how people switch off from work is the atmosphere at work: conflicts, gossiping and back-stabbing are corrosive and draining and should be avoided at all costs. If someone gossips to you about a work colleague behind their back they are bound to do the same to you. Back-stabbing always leaves a nasty atmosphere at work; and you may end up worrying about what you have said instead of trying to unwind in your leisure time. You can never have complete control over your work (and it would be a strange place to work if you did); however, you do have the ability to significantly reduce the chances of experiencing stress by the conscious choices you make every day at work. Therefore, don't gossip — lecture over!

Make time to socialise

It is good to have a regular group of people with whom you feel comfortable hanging around. It is good to have someone to offload on. I once interviewed a head teacher for a project I was working on and she explained to me her own inimitable way of dealing with the stress of being the head of a large primary school. She couldn't drive, and it was difficult to commute home by train as she lived about seventy-five minutes away and the connections were not that great. Each day her husband, who did drive, collected her from work on his way home. She said that as soon as she got into the car she vented her stress and her emotions of the day. Because her husband was concentrating on driving he didn't pay that much attention, apart from the odd nod or grunt. She was aware of this, but she nevertheless found it helped to share her frustrations, and, once out of the car, they both felt they could relax and enjoy a pleasant evening away from work.

Set boundaries

Sometimes in the work environment the line between friends and colleagues can become blurred. Try to avoid revealing too much about your personal life in the workplace. Not only is this unprofessional, it will also change the perception your colleagues have about you. A little bit of mystery is a good thing. Once you know who the wizard is behind the curtain, the illusion is lost. Thus it is best in the long run to keep your personal and professional worlds apart. Don't let your career invade your personal space, and by the same token don't open your personal life to all at work. It is not always easy to keep these worlds entirely separate, but striving for the balance will help you stay sane, and hopefully to thrive in both worlds.

It is also very important to develop friendships away from work. While there is no real problem with having work colleagues who are also your friends outside work, if your workmates are the only friends you have this makes it extremely difficult to escape from work. If you socialise with a co-worker your conversation will inevitably drift back to work. I am not saying that you should never see your work colleagues outside work. Now and again, it is good to go out for a bonding session or to let off steam with your workmates. It is, however, difficult if something goes wrong at work and you become the focus of gossip or you have to make a difficult decision, and your workmates turn their backs on you. It is, though, very good to have at least one person at work who you feel you can confide in, be honest with and whose judgement you really respect and trust. Trust is very important as you do not want your dirty linen being aired in public. Emails make it too easy to spread gossip around the office, so be careful when sending emails. Any work email can potentially be read out in court, so check before you send. If your email is a rant, put it in the drafts folder first and wait a few hours to read again before sending.

Develop a positive attitude towards your work and your colleagues; it is an absolute joy to work in an organisation with good colleagues. Find something positive in your work — being positive makes a big difference. Find people who think like you, who are prepared to go that extra mile, and tell people when they have overstepped the boundaries. It is very rewarding if you are lucky enough to find like-minded individuals who share similar goals and ambitions, and who leave their egos at home. Being sarcastic about everything, every new idea, every change or way of working is not good for health and wellbeing, and this will be noticed by your line manager. It will also feed into your leisure time. 'Why should I bother, this won't work.' You can develop positivity by being around positive people but you can also develop negativity and cynicism by being around negative people. Surrounding yourself with negative people makes you feel negative and down. It is all too easy to be cynical but before long this starts to rub off on you and it will affect your productivity. Finally, if you repeatedly go home thinking about all the negative issues at work — instead of reflecting about the good day you had — it is probably time to consider a different role within the organisation, or leave your present employer.

25
Working
from home

'He is the happiest, be he king or peasant,
who finds peace in his home'

Goethe

It is becoming more common for people to work from home. They do so for a number of reasons. One in five employees say that, given the choice, they would work from home as least some of the time. Traditionally, home working used to be the domain of the cottage-industry worker, or the self-employed, but thanks to advances in technology it is becoming more and more common today for people to work from home.

One in five employees prefer working from home

The pros and cons of working from home

There are plenty of advantages from working at home for both the employer and their employees. As an employee, it is convenient: you do not have to dress in your corporate clothes, you can choose when to take a break and you can complete some of your household or domestic chores around your working day. People who work at home often say they are more productive as they can concentrate on a particular piece of work or project without the usual day-to-day interruptions at the office. Some say they can focus better at home as they are not being distracted by other people. I have known people to say they actually work harder from home as they do not want to be seen to be taking it easy. Nonetheless, most people report they are happier having the flexibility to be able to work from home as they report a better work/life balance.

Home working also has a number of benefits for the employer. Staff retention is higher, as employees are happier and less stressed, there is higher morale in the workforce, and employees report greater loyalty and commitment from their staff. In terms of cost, home working also reduces overheads, the need for office space, etc. It is also good for the corporate brand: a company that offers home working is seen as being a flexible, dynamic, forward-thinking employer.

Flexible working suits many employees' needs and brings many benefits both to the employer and employee. However, there are downsides. Some people feel isolated by home working, especially if they are naturally social people or they live on their own. Another issue I am often reminded of is that some people who work from home don't feel any escape from work. If your workplace is your home, you are constantly being exposed to cues about work.

Dress for work but stay at home

I once interviewed a man who worked at home. He told me that he had an interesting strategy for helping him unwind at the end of the working day. As he worked at home there was no natural physical boundary to distance him from work. He didn't need to cycle, drive or take the train to work, as his office was located in a spare room. As crazy as it sounds, this man dressed for work. He shaved, showered and put on his suit as if he was going to the office. In his office he had a separate phone for work calls. At the end of the day he immediately changed and either went into his garden or to a different room in the house. He never — unless he absolutely had to — went back in his office during the evening.

Another example I read about concerned a priest who lived in the grounds of her church. In order to separate work and home life she had an archway constructed between her garden and the church grounds with a solid wooden gate; and as she went through the gate this marked the end of her working day and the beginning of her leisure time. Thus, the physical boundary also acted as a psychological boundary separating her two worlds.

A few tips for successful home working

If you work from home and you find it difficult to escape from work during your leisure time, the following techniques may help you to unwind.

- Try to keep your working environment completely separate from your home environment. I know that sometimes this is not that easy.
- If you have an office at home, close the door when you have finished for the day.

- Don't leave work folders, laptop, paperwork, reports, etc., lying around the house on display as these will only trigger work-related thoughts.
- Try to set up a routine. I know one of the joys of home working is that it frees your time so you can start and finish when you wish, but I strongly recommend that you develop a fixed routine and stick to it. Treat your day as any other working day or the time will evaporate, and you may end up working in the evening just to catch up.
- Plan meal times and breaks and set a time limit for each.
- Never switch on the television during the day.
- Don't be tempted to do any leisure activities during your working day (unless you decide to give yourself a mental break and a boost by going for a jog or cycle ride). Save these activities until you have finished and give yourself a reward.
- Go for a walk at the end of the working day or go to the gym.
- Have a shower at the end of your day.

IV

Nurture yourself to develop resilience

Overview

In previous chapters we discussed exercises and techniques you can use to help you unwind from work in order to relax the mind. This final part is concerned with developing resilience. Building up your resilience (to stress) can really help you switch off better, and having a relaxed mind can help you handle the challenges work throws you. There are two main aims in this final part. The first is concerned with developing good physical health. In terms of physical health I present chapters on sleep, exercise and nutrition. Healthier people are better equipped to deal with the day-to-day demands of work. I don't go into too much detail here as there are numerous books devoted to this subject. When we become busy it is all too easy to neglect our own needs, and sleep, exercise and nutrition tend to take a back seat. If this happens our resilience dips.

In the final chapter, therefore, I discuss why it is important to monitor, revise and take stock on a regular basis. Included in this chapter is a measure you can complete so you can easily spot when you are pushing yourself too much. You need to pace and nurture yourself, as you can only boost resilience by nurturing your own needs. By attending to our own needs, and making time for activities we enjoy, we can protect our health. Developing resilience takes time, and it is easy to become discouraged when things don't go as planned. Indeed, setbacks are to be expected and in the final chapter I discuss what to do when pressures build up and how to bounce back and move on when hiccups occur.

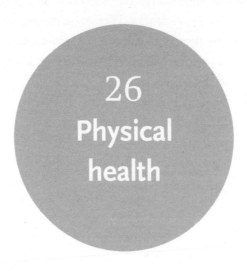

26
Physical
health

'A long healthy life is no accident. It begins with good genes, but it also depends on good habits'

Dan Buettner

If you ask people to list the most important things in life, not surprisingly health ranks quite high. Staying healthy is one of the most important things you can do for yourself and your family and friends. Most of us take our health for granted. I have never spoken to anyone who said they would rather be unhealthy, but isn't it strange how so many people seem to go out of their way to make themselves ill? Approximately 64 per cent of the UK adult population are overweight (69 per cent in the USA), 18.5 per cent smoke, 30 per cent do not get enough sleep and nearly 40 per cent do little or no physical activity/exercise.

Apart from managing stress and learning to relax, I think there are three key activities to achieving and maintaining good physical health: cardiovascular exercise, good nutrition and good sleep. The next chapter is devoted entirely to sleep, so in this one I shall discuss eating and exercise. I treat them under separate headings, although they are all connected in various ways as exercise is also very good for sleep, and certain food types are better for exercise and aiding sleep. There are many (some say too many) books and websites dedicated to food, nutrition and exercise, and therefore I will not be covering these topics in great deal. The aim of this chapter is really to encourage you to think about your health, since being healthy will aid the unwinding from work process.

Physical activity

In order for an employee to cope with the demands of work and to perform at an optimal level during work, they not only need to regulate their behaviour both inside and outside of work, they also need to achieve a certain level of fitness. Being fit and healthy helps to build up resilience that we need to cope with the demands of work, and engaging in sport or exercise has been shown to increase positive mood and wellbeing. Moreover, compared to unfit individuals, fit people tend to recover more quickly from the physical demands of work. Participating in sporting activities is also an excellent way to switch off mentally.

There is an overwhelming body of evidence to demonstrate the benefits of regular exercise. Physical exercising and physical fitness are associated with increased vigour, positive mood, improved concentration and mental resilience, and a reduction in anxiety and depression. Being fit has also been shown to help us deal with stress. There is also a large body of research showing the biological/physiological benefits of taking regular exercise, such as the lowering of blood pressure and resting heart rate, lowering the risk of cardiovascular disease, stroke and increasing immune functioning, bone density and blood sugar regulation.

The recommended guidelines suggest we should aim to exercise for at least thirty minutes a day at least five times a week. Exercise need not be done in a thirty-minute block, so, if you are just starting out, as little as ten minutes' exercise has been found to be beneficial. However, as you improve and become fitter you may like to increase the time you spend exercising. One reason people don't stick to exercise regimes is that often they push themselves too hard too quickly. If you haven't exercised for a while, take it really easy for the first month and gradually build up the time you cycle, jog or swim. For example, if you choose swimming, give yourself a rest after each length and don't do too many lengths. Once you have completed an exercise session you should feel refreshed but you should not feel too drained or fatigued. If you do, this suggests you have pushed yourself too much. However, it is important to consult a health professional before undertaking an exercise programme. When people push themselves too far too soon they quickly become disillusioned with exercise and give up. This is why it is important to take it easy early on. In addition, remember to warm up (and down) slowly before you exercise so as to avoid injury and strain.

People often confuse thinness with good health. In a series of studies in the USA,[1] Steven Blair has convincingly demonstrated that fitness is more important for health and wellbeing than leanness, that is, being thin. In one study Blair and colleagues followed up people for approximately eight years. At the beginning of the study some 8,000 people were given a full exercise stress test to establish their level of fitness. Over the intervening period 143 people died of cancer and 144 from cardiovascular disease. The team divided the sample into those who were thin, those who were normal weight and those who were obese, and examined the risk of death in relation to body mass and physical fitness. Essentially this meant there were six groups: fit people (lean, normal, obese) and unfit (lean, normal, obese). They used the fit people of normal weight as their reference group. Not too unsurprisingly, those who were obese and unfit were seven times more likely to die of cardiovascular disease over the eight-year period than normal, fit people. Also not too unsurprisingly, the fit lean people were less likely to die of cardiovascular disease, relative to the normal-weight fit people. However, the unfit lean people were approximately 3.5 times more likely to die relative to the fit normal-weight people, but incredibly the obese but fit people were only two times more likely to die of cardiovascular disease. Thus, those who appeared to be most at risk were the obese and lean unfit group. It didn't matter if you were thin or fat, the most important factor for reducing the risk of cardiovascular disease in this study was being fit! These are incredible findings and I hope they are sufficiently convincing to encourage you (if you don't already exercise) to start exercising. One final point: a similar pattern of results were found when the researchers also examined the risk of dying from cancer.

Make time for exercise. Physical activity can be incorporated into your daily life in a number of ways. People can become more physically active by participating in sporting activities. Maybe you could join a sports club and then you can also enjoy the social benefits of meeting people. However, you don't necessarily need to join a gym in order to get fit as you can incorporate physical activity into your daily routines. For example, you could cycle to work if you live a reasonable distance from work and it is safe to cycle. You could take the train and walk from the station instead of taking the car, or you could also do simple things such as taking the staircase instead of the lift. Aim to incorporate physical activity into your daily life and such activity will soon become routine. With a little bit of effort and planning, you will soon reap the benefits. As stated above, always consult a health professional before undertaking an exercise programme.

Eating

Food is essential for survival and we take this for granted. Eating the correct type of food is nonetheless essential to build energy levels and strengthen immune functioning. There is an expression, you are what you eat, and I do believe that what you eat affects the way we feel, function and perform. Eating the right type of foods can boost your immune system, improve your circulation and can help you to maintain your blood sugar levels. In a nutshell, eating the right type of food can help us to deal with and fight off the effects of stress and infection. Certain food types, for example cranberries and blueberries, are recognised as boosting cognition and reaction times. Conversely, eating the wrong types of foods, e.g. eating too much saturated fat, consuming too much caffeine, salt and sugars, or eating too many large meals, can be damaging to health.

I think most people are aware of the beneficial effects of eating fresh fruit and vegetables and whole grains. Fresh fruit and vegetables contain various vitamins, minerals, enzymes and nutrients that are essential for good health. And many foods contain antioxidants that are reported to be effective in preventing a range of age-related diseases, including cardiovascular disease, cancer and Alzheimer's disease. These are literally disease-fighting agents, and the best place to get them is fresh produce. Many fruit and vegetables are rich in antioxidants; those with bright, distinctive colours, such as tomatoes, blueberries, corn and carrots are particularly beneficial. However, green, leafy vegetables like kale, collards and spinach, green tea, citrus fruits and apples and pears are also considered a good source of antioxidants.

Antioxidants provide benefits by removing free radicals from our bloodstream. As we age our bodily tissue suffers from a natural process called oxidation. This occurs when molecules in our bodies lose electrons to electrically charged molecules (called free radicals) of oxygen in our bloodstream. Free radicals have the potential to damage cellular DNA, and over time this can become irreversible, leading to disease. A diet rich in antioxidants is thought necessary to moderate the level of free radicals in our bodies, and therefore essential to maintaining good health.

Don't go to work with an empty tank

How does the saying go? 'Breakfast like a king!'? Breakfast is often regarded as the most important meal of the day, and dinner the most enjoyable. A good breakfast sets us up for the day, and dinner is something we look forward to at the end of it. Try to eat a balanced diet. Breakfast foods that release energy slowly are thought to be particularly beneficial as they seem to fill us up for longer and reduce the likelihood of us craving food or experiencing an energy dip. Unfortunately there is a fashion these days for people to skip breakfast at home and grab a takeaway coffee along with a sugary pastry on the way to work. As an occasional treat, this is fine, but it is probably not good in the long run. Also drink plenty of fluids throughout the day to prevent dehydration.

Although for most breakfast may be the mandatory bowl of yoghurt and a round of toast, many people plan and like to prepare their evening meal. Poor old lunch hardly gets a look in and most people will rush through lunch grabbing a quick sandwich just to load up on calories to see them through to the evening and prevent hunger pangs. Even when eating alone many people hardly notice the food they eat, as they are busy looking at the internet, checking emails or browsing.

Many don't realise the benefits of the lunch break. I think we have lost our perspective about the lunch break. Lunch gives us time to slow down and take stock of what we have been doing and where we want to go. If we bury ourselves in work, and don't come up for air during the day by taking breaks, we will find it more difficult to unwind during the evening. You need to take your foot off the accelerator now and again during the day. If we continually focus on the task at hand, we lose the ability to plan strategically and see things in the broader context.

Some senior managers are, however, beginning to realise the importance of having time to reflect during the working day. In researching a book, Frank Partnoy, a professor of law and finance at the University of San Diego, said that 'he was struck by how many senior leaders stressed the importance of strategic "downtime" — lunch or some other block of an hour or more per day — to break up their thinking and spur them to be more strategic'. It is interesting how many time or stress management books argue the opposite and how important it is to squeeze in as many activities and get things done at every opportunity. Why waste time on a sixty-minute lunch when you can wolf down a sandwich in five minutes!

People who skip or miss their breaks are often not as productive as their colleagues. By sitting back and reflecting, you will be in a better position to see the larger picture and surprised about how much more work you are getting done. One employee I spoke to said that she goes to the office gym in her lunchtime, and that this lunchtime workout, as well as keeping her healthy, helps her to focus better for the rest of the day.

Make lunch mandatory: put it in your diary as an appointment with yourself

In a study of transit operators including bus drivers, light rail, street and cable car operators and conductors, researchers from the Prevention Research Center, University of California, interviewed and gave questionnaires to 1,208 respondents about their daily problems at work, supervisory support, meals and alcohol consumption. In addition interviewees were asked about the length of time it took them to unwind and relax after work. Skipping meals and daily job problems increased the length of time to unwind or were associated with an increased difficulty in unwinding after work.

Many people work through lunch because they believe they can get more done. This is the wrong attitude. It may feel as if you are getting caught up with work but it will only increase fatigue levels later in the afternoon. Use your lunch break to recharge your batteries. To use a sporting analogy: a good sportsperson knows that rest is just as important as training, and their coach/trainer will build in rest periods within their training schedule. Many people who are keen on a particular sport, say running or cycling, will also spend time doing a different sport, say swimming, as although they are both cardiovascular they use different muscle groups. One primarily uses the legs while the other uses the arms. Also they may decide to do weight training one day instead of cardiovascular work. Thus, cross-training, as it is called, prevents strain due to the overuse of a particular muscle group. It also helps to keep sportsmen and women motivated as well as preventing injury and burnout. Similarly some people advocate the left-brain/right-brain theory. The basic idea is that the two sides of our brain are suited to different types of tasks. The left side is very good for critical thinking, language, logic and reasoning, while the right side is good for colour, creativity, expressing and reading emotions, intuition, music, and recognising faces. Thus, the left side of the brain is considered the analytical/logical side, and the right the emotional/creative side. As in cross-training, if you have been working on a problem that involves the left side of the brain, such as critical thinking, it may be good to switch to a task that requires the right side; for example, one that requires you to be creative, or even listening to some music (you can do this during your lunch break). This is why listening to music can aid relaxation and recuperation. However, the research literature is not completely clear on this issue, as current thinking would suggest that the brain works better when both halves work together, as in mathematics, but it does seem to make intuitive sense for preventing fatigue, and many people actively use this method of task switching.

Your health should be your top priority no matter what else is going on in your life. If we are healthy, we feel good about ourselves, we are less of a burden to our families and friends and the State. Moreover, being healthy seems to make us happier, and gives us the strength and resources to deal with what life throws at us. It is draining to deal with demanding work tasks but it is more difficult if you are unfit and unwell. A fit person will also be able to enjoy their leisure time more, as they will not be as tired and fatigued from work as an unfit person. It is really not that hard to look after yourself — it is certainly not rocket science — but it does require some thought, planning and dedication to get healthy and then to maintain your health. We should all make being healthy a priority.

27
Sleep

'Fatigue is the safest sleeping draught'
Virginia Woolf, *Jacob's Room*

In 2011, the then chief executive of Lloyds Banking Group, Antonio Horta-Osório, was forced to relinquish his duties and take sick leave. On Monday 31 October 2011, the successful forty-seven-year-old banker had a meeting with Lloyds chairman Sir Win Bischoff to explain why he couldn't carry on for the moment. He told Sir Win that he hadn't been able to sleep for five days. He is quoted as saying:

> *'The week before I was sleeping less and less. I asked the chairman if I could take three days off because I wanted to rest and sleep. I took those three days and went to Lisbon and actually I didn't rest at all. I couldn't sleep. I couldn't switch off.'*

It is not surprising Horta-Osório took time off work due to the effects of not sleeping.

Sleep

Sleep takes up a major part of our twenty-four-hour day and we spend approximately a third of our lives sleeping, so there must be a good reason why we have evolved to sleep.

Sleep is considered to be the most important recovery mechanism available to man, and therefore good sleep is essential for optimal wellbeing, daily functioning and health. Sleep loss and sleep disturbance can lead to performance deficits, fatigue, mood changes and in extreme cases even impaired immune function. It is assumed that sleep must be continuous to enable the body to restore itself. Sleep has also been associated with life expectancy and some people think sleep may be more influential in terms of longevity than diet, exercise or genetics, although the research is not completely consistent in this respect.

It is easy to confuse tiredness/sleepiness with fatigue. Sleepiness/tiredness is the tendency or the need to fall asleep. Fatigue is our physiological response to prolonged sleep loss or prolonged physical or mental exertion. Fatigue may be reduced by sedentary activity, or rest without sleeping, whereas subjective sleepiness and the propensity for sleep are often exacerbated by sedentary activity or rest. Sleepiness is something we normally experience on a weekend when we choose to have a lazy day. We somehow feel more tired by not doing anything.

Five sleep stages

When sleeping, we go through cycles of five sleep stages: four stages of Non-Rapid Eye Movement (NREM) sleep, and one stage of Rapid Eye Movement (REM) sleep. Each cycle lasts between five minutes and one and a half hours. Stage 1 sleep is a transitional stage lasting approximately five minutes, where the body prepares itself for sleep. It is a state of drowsiness and if woken up during this stage the person may not feel that they have been to sleep at all. Stage 2 sleep is a light sleep stage where brain activity, heart rate and breathing slow down and muscle tension is reduced. Sleep becomes progressively deeper through stages 3 and 4 (sometimes known as slow-wave sleep) and it is thought that the body has the opportunity to refresh and rejuvenate itself during stage 4. This stage is good for memory and it is thought our memories are consolidated in this state. If you wake people during stage 4 sleep they have difficulty remembering what they have learnt earlier in the day. People then return to the lighter stage of sleep (stage 2) before entering REM sleep (stage 5). This stage of sleep is characterised by rapid eye movements as if the person is awake, and brain activity, heart rate and breathing rate all increase in this stage. This is the stage where most dreaming occurs and the brain processes and stores new information to aid long-term memory. It has been suggested that the brain blocks signals to the muscles in this stage to prevent people from acting out their dreams. This cycle of sleep stages is repeated approximately five times over the course of the night. The length of the sleep stages also changes over the course of the night with most deep sleep (stages 3 and 4) occurring at the beginning of the night and more REM sleep towards the end of the night.

How much sleep is needed?

People vary in their sleep needs. Some people prefer to sleep for nine or more hours daily, while others manage to function relatively well on less than six hours per night.

Calvin Coolidge, the thirtieth President of the United States, was well known for being a long sleeper. Coolidge would sleep eight hours or more, most nights, and he would normally take an additional two to three hours' sleep in the afternoon. He is recorded as having more sleep in his time in the White House than any other president. It has been said (and as with most good stories there is probably a grain of truth in it) that his very first act when he became president was to go to sleep!

By contrast, Margaret Thatcher, the first female British Prime Minister, was said to thrive on four hours' sleep per night when she was in office. This fact was widely known by her cabinet ministers and equally widely reported in the media. This added to the myth of the 'Iron Lady'. It is said that her reputation for only needing four hours' sleep led to a competitive behaviour between her party to see who could sleep the least; so-called 'sleeporexia'. There are not actually that many people who can function well with only four hours' sleep a night. Without sufficient sleep people become fatigued and accumulate sleep debt. Napping is a way most people compensate for lack of sleep. There is an interesting picture of Margaret Thatcher dozing at the Conservative Youth conference in Eastbourne in 1975.

The sleep industry is worth over $20 billion

The pursuit of the perfect sleep has become a multi-billion-pound industry — five years ago, *Forbes* estimated it as worth some $20 billion — as we invest in pillows, mattresses, sleep clinics, herbal tinctures, hypnotherapy and, of course, sleeping tablets.

Before the invention of electricity people slept for nine to ten hours per night

On average, people in the Western world sleep for approximately seven to nine hours per night. However, sleep needs vary considerably across the age span and from one individual to another. It is interesting that within less than a couple of centuries our sleeping habits have changed dramatically. Before electricity, people slept for approximately nine to ten hours per night. Today, therefore, we are having less than the amount of sleep we need, suggesting that most of us have built up a 'sleep debt'.

We all have our own natural thresholds concerning the number of hours' sleep we need. Some people need more, others less. If we don't get enough sleep we develop a 'sleep debt' and like all debt this needs to be repaid. Most of us can do this reasonably easily with a lie-in at the weekend but there are many people who are chronically sleep-deprived. Sleep researchers believe many people in Western societies are chronically sleep-deprived, and it is easy to see why. In the USA, the number of people who report they sleep six hours or less most nights increased from 13 per cent in 1999 to 20 per cent in 2009. This is slightly worrying considering that sleep deprivation is associated with reduced alertness, task performance, decision-making capacity, occupational injuries and wellbeing. It is well known, and we don't have to reiterate this, that many accidents are caused by sleep debt. Tasks that require innovative thinking or strategic planning are certainly performed better with adequate sleep.

In 2010 the American Psychological Association reported the results of a survey that found 70 per cent of Americans perceived work to be a 'significant' or very significant cause of stress. It has also been estimated that between 29 and 45 per cent of the adult population may experience some form of sleep disturbance. There are many reasons for this but perhaps the invention and the availability of electricity is a contributory factor as we are now exposed to artificial light and stimulation in the evening.

Although sleep need varies between individuals — some people can get by on relatively little — most people need seven and half to eight and a half hours a night. Don't feel guilty about needing more than eight hours' sleep. There is no absolute set sleep time and people do vary. Sometimes this creates issues in relationships where one partner needs lots of sleep and the other not so much. Remember, one of the greatest scientific minds of all time, Albert Einstein, was said to sleep around ten hours a night. This was unless he was working on a particularly hard topic — then he would need eleven hours!

To nap or not to nap: that is the question

Some life coaches will often talk about napping. In the nineties the idea of the power nap was born, the idea being that a short nap, between fifteen and thirty minutes, restores wakefulness and promotes performance and learning. Unless absolutely essential — that is, if you feel too tired to function safely — I think napping should be avoided. People only nap because they have sleep debt. Napping should not be used to supplement abnormal sleep. There is evidence that workers actually sleep worse on Sunday evenings if they take a nap during the day. Thus, people tend to nap because they have accumulated a sleep deficit. Conversely, napping or sleeping for more than thirty minutes appears to be associated with impaired alertness following awakening, and this feeling, called sleep inertia, can last quite a while before the individual feels able to perform at a normal level.

Many people who have difficulty switching off from work also have trouble with sleeping because they find themselves thinking about and going over and over work issues while in bed. This can result in difficulty in getting to sleep, maintaining sleep, or waking up too early in the morning and not getting back to sleep. In my research I speak to many people who say they have sleep problems.

Rachel, for example, came to see me because she had difficulty sleeping and said that she would lie awake and her mind would go over and over. She told me that she didn't understand it because she could easily fall asleep on the sofa in the evenings while watching television but not when she went to bed. She said she would lie in bed getting more and more frustrated and she would start worrying that if she didn't get enough sleep she would not be able to function at work the next day. She also said that she noticed she became very irritable.

Rachel's sleeping problems were quite easy to solve. Her main issue was napping in front of the television; this suggested to me that she could fall asleep quite easily. The reason she couldn't get to sleep in bed later in the evening was because she was by then less tired and her mind would start to wander. We developed a sleep hygiene routine (see steps below), which meant putting an end to her evening napping and we also worked on a plan for her to develop a regular bedtime routine. Within a couple of weeks Rachel was no longer complaining about her mind wandering at bedtime, and she was sleeping much better and (to the relief of her partner and friends) was less irritable.

One train of thought championed by Dale Carnegie was 'If you can't sleep, then get up and do something instead of lying there and worrying. It's the worry that gets you, not the loss of sleep.' This was clearly practised by one of our clients, Tony. His sleep was affected and he had on occasion resorted to working in the early hours of the morning.

Tony, a high ruminator who had profound difficulty switching off and unwinding from work, said:

'When you go to sleep you wake up … I've actually come down, logged on to the server at two o'clock in the morning and done some work … but if you do that for an hour, then you could be quite tired. But if you solve the problem to a certain extent then you can remove the problem from your head. So the hour of lost sleep and work

*you've just done often means you can go back up … and just turn
off and get to sleep. If you didn't do anything you could be lying
there with the thought still running through your head.'*

Unfortunately, however, this sets up an accepted behaviour pattern
in your own mind and before long you will find it will become a
habit. This is, therefore, why this is not something I recommend.

Sleep debt can have very serious consequences

We often relate the effects of sleep deprivation to high-profile
accidents. For example, there have been a number of tragic, high-
profile accidents which were thought to have been down to human
fatigue, caused in part by sleep loss — the *Exxon Valdez* oil spill off
Alaska in 1989, and the Selby rail crash in Yorkshire in 2001 spring
all too readily to mind. Sleep deprivation and sleepiness also play
a significant role in many less prominent but nevertheless serious
accidents. In the USA a crane operator dozed off during a break,
and when he woke, half dazed, he opened the door on the wrong
side of his cab and fell thirty-five feet to his death. It was said this
was after he had worked his third of three consecutive thirteen-
hour shifts.

Sleep longer and improve your sex life

Poor sleep can affect us in other ways. Research suggests that sleeping
between six and seven hours per night increases the risk of becoming
obese. That is, people who regularly sleep less than seven hours per
night are around 30 per cent more likely to be obese compared to
people who get nine hours. Continued poor sleep quality is associated

with decreased immunity, and poor sleepers are at a greater risk to developing colds. And, finally, sleep restriction has been associated with a reduced sex drive in both men and women. It appears that some people are just too tired to have sex.

Don't waste your weekends sleeping in

Unfortunately, many of us are not aware that even moderate sleep loss is associated with reduced alertness. A number of carefully controlled laboratory studies have clearly demonstrated that six hours of sleep or less over a sustained period of time leads to dramatic decrements in vigilance and performance. Sleep curtailment not only affects our performance; sleeping is a period of recovery not just for the brain but for the body. Blood pressure and heart rate decline during sleep, reflecting changes in the autonomic nervous system that accompany sleep. Sleep restriction leads to changes in the regulation of blood glucose and insulin.

As a society, our sleep debt is partly a direct consequence of our 24/7 lifestyle. People simply don't sleep long enough. We tend to stay up late watching television or doing other activities, and delay the time we go to bed. This is OK if you can catch up with your sleep at the weekends, although it seems a shame that you spend a good portion of your quality free time sleeping when you could simply have gone to bed earlier in the week. Other sleep problems and sleep disorders may not be related to the timing of sleep but to work- (or family-related stress or worries. In fact, one of the major causes of sleep onset latency — how long it takes to fall asleep — is worry. How we think and feel affects how long it takes to fall asleep. We have shown in numerous studies that people who have difficulty switching off from work during the evening and at bedtime are on average four times more likely to report problems in trying to fall asleep, and seven times more likely to report restless sleep during the night compared to individuals who are able to unwind during their evening leisure time.

Assessing sleep

When we consider sleep, we typically distinguish between sleep quantity and sleep quality. Sleep quantity refers to how long we sleep, and a relatively simple measure of sleep quantity is what we call 'sleep efficient index'. This refers to how long we sleep relative to how long we spend in bed, and it is quite easy to calculate. To calculate your own sleep efficiency work out your total sleep time, divided by the total time in bed, and then times by 100. This will produce a percentage value. For example, if you slept for 7 hours last night but spent 8 hours in bed (7/8 hours) x 100 = 87.5 per cent. You can use the table on the next page to help you work out your sleep efficiency index. A general rule of thumb is that normal sleep is anything over 85 per cent. A number of factors can reduce sleep efficiency, such as noise, temperature, needing to go to the bathroom frequently, being disturbed by your partner or children, or experiencing a racing mind caused by worrying about work issues. Thus, anything that causes you to have a restless night will reduce your sleep efficiency index.

To assess the amount of sleep you get, complete the table on the next page.

	Hours	Minutes
1. When did you go to bed?	☐	☐
2. What time did the lights go out?	☐	☐
3. How long did it take you to fall asleep?	☐	☐
4. What time did you wake up?	☐	☐
5. What time did you get out of bed?	☐	☐
6. How long did you sleep?	☐	☐
Total sleep time	☐	☐

For some reason, many people I speak to don't make the link between going to bed late and feeling tired in the mornings. Listen to your body. If you are tired during the day, try going to bed a little earlier. Remember the old saying: an hour before midnight is worth two hours after. I guess in their own minds to many people 11.30 may not seem that late, but it is if you are tired and fighting the natural urge to sleep.

You may be thinking to yourself that surely it is not how long you sleep but how you feel on awakening, and this is why it is important to consider sleep quality. Sleep quality is your subjective experience of sleep, and how refreshed you feel in the morning is a clear indication of how you have slept. Sleep is very individualistic and some people require more sleep than others. Look at the table on the next page and circle the number that best describes your sleep experience over the last two weeks.

Think about the questions in terms of your sleep over the previous few nights.

	Very easy			Very difficult	
Was it difficult or easy to fall asleep?	1	2	3	4	5
Once asleep was it difficult to stay asleep?	1	2	3	4	5
If you awoke during the night, how easy or difficult was it to get back to sleep?	1	2	3	4	5
	Very calm			Very restless	
Was your sleep restless or calm?	1	2	3	4	5
	Very well			Very poorly	
How did you sleep?	1	2	3	4	5
	Totally			Not at all	
How refreshed did you feel on awakening?	1	2	3	4	5

By completing the table you should be able to see whether your sleep is disturbed throughout the night (question 1) or whether your difficulties specifically relate to sleep onset issues (questions 2, 3, 4 and 5). Sleep onset insomnia is trouble *falling* asleep, and sleep maintenance insomnia is trouble *staying* asleep. People who have sleep maintenance insomnia may find they wake several times during the night. Both types can leave you feeling unrefreshed in the morning (question 5). A total score over the whole table of more than eighteen over a number of nights suggests that you do have a sleeping issue.

If you have difficulty falling asleep this could be due to a number of reasons, and if you can't get to sleep that easily your mind will invariably start to go over issues that have been affecting you recently, such as work. Practising the exercises in Parts II and III of this book will help in this respect. However, your first line of defence is to ensure that you are following what we call basic sleep hygiene principles. I have laid these out below.

Everyone wakes up during the night but most of us are not consciously aware when it happens and we normally fall back to sleep without much difficulty. Moreover, we don't even remember waking up. These short periods of awakening don't constitute a sleep issue and rarely trouble us. If, however, something has been bothering us at work, we may find ourselves waking up during the night and replaying the event over and over in our minds. Even if we only wake to use the bathroom, we may start thinking about work issues.

We all have the occasional rough night's sleep and when this happens we just have to tough it out and get on with it. We have probably all on occasion woken up during the night and thought about a work issue or something else that has been bothering us. This is annoying and it may make us irritable and sluggish the next day, and we will probably have more difficulty concentrating, but it will not harm us. It is only when we do this on a regular basis and it becomes persistent and affects our wellbeing that we need to take action. Therefore, don't worry if you have the occasional troubled night. Just tough it out and carry on.

The key to a good night's sleep

Some individuals find it difficult to switch off from work-related thoughts during the evening and lie in bed thinking about work-related issues. When this happens it is therefore necessary for you to find ways to distract yourself from these thoughts — pursuing hobbies during the evening will be beneficial in this respect. Train yourself to park the thought (as discussed in chapter 18). Listed below are some tips to help you achieve a good night's sleep.

- Regular bedtime routines with consistent sleep and wake times. Develop a consistent sleep and wake time. You don't need to be too rigid here to the point of becoming obsessional, but a key to good sleep is developing a consistent routine. Your body will adapt and will start to prepare itself for sleep. Try not to sleep in too late at the weekend.

- Don't work too late in the evening.

- Distract yourself from work.

- Take regular breaks during the day and don't skip lunch.
  One young woman I interviewed told me that on days when she misses her lunch and rest breaks because of back-to-back meetings she finds it more difficult to unwind and sleep during these evenings, despite feeling more fatigued than usual. Sometimes the body gets overtired but the brain becomes over-aroused.

- Limit your caffeine intake.
  Caffeine is a stimulant and can lead to poor sleep quality, particularly if ingested close to bedtime. Caffeine intake has also been associated with increased arousal so individuals should limit the number of cups of tea and coffee they consume over the day. Also there are many caffeine-containing foods and beverages such as chocolate and cola, and these often contain a significant amount of caffeine; and most of the time we consume these products without being aware of their caffeine content. Even moderate amounts of caffeine can affect sleep. In one study,[1] adult men were given a single 200mg dose of caffeine (equivalent to one to two cups of regular coffee) or a non-active placebo before 7.30 in the morning. They consumed no more caffeine products for the remainder of the day. The results showed that, on the day participants were given the caffeine, they experienced delayed sleep onset, and over the night they had reduced sleep; a clear demonstration that even a relatively small

dose of caffeine can have a considerable effect on sleep. You may consider yourself one of those lucky people who can drink coffee all day and during the evening and still sleep well. However, this may be because your body has become addicted to caffeine. In any case consuming too much caffeine is not good for us.

- Dim the lights thirty minutes before you go to bed.
  Dimming the lights half an hour before you go to bed will over time train your mind into believing that you will be going to sleep soon. Also, light exposure suppresses the production of melatonin, the hormone secreted by the pineal gland that helps to regulate sleep/wake cycles. Melatonin secretion increases subjective sleepiness, and decreases core body temperature. Therefore try to avoid any bright lights prior to bedtime, and make your bedroom as free from any artificial light as possible.

- Don't look at smartphones or tablets while you are in bed.
  The backlight given off by many smartphones and tablets has been shown to suppress the production of melatonin, resulting in delayed sleep onset. As stated earlier, try not to engage with your smartphone or tablet devices in the last hour before going to bed.

- The bedroom environment.
  It is important that the bedroom environment is conducive to sleeping, that the person establishes a regular bedtime routine and does not bring a laptop, mobile phone, television, etc., into the bedroom! The bedroom should be associated with sleep and sex. If you wake up during the night and see your laptop or diary this will more than likely evoke memories of work. Also it is not good practice to have clocks on display as this only encourages us to watch the clock, and you will get frustrated and start to worry if you see the minutes ticking by and you can't get to sleep.

- Don't chastise or punish yourself.

  Sometimes people punish themselves for not getting to sleep quickly. They become angry, tense and frustrated with themselves for lying there not sleeping. They may use self-blame ruminative responses, for example, 'I am useless, I can't sleep', 'Why can't I sleep?', 'What if I never fall asleep?', 'How am I going to cope with work tomorrow?' Their mind begins to spiral out of control. 'If I don't get my eight hours' sleep tonight I will not be able to do my work in the morning.' Such thinking only raises anxiety and tension and contributes to you getting even poorer sleep. If this happens you need to remind yourself that you can function with only a few hours' sleep if it is for only one night. You may be a little tired but you should be fine. Try to distract yourself by thinking of something pleasant, a holiday you have had, or think about your fantasy. It doesn't really matter what you think about so long as it distracts you from your work-related thoughts. Never, never, punish yourself for not sleeping.

- In the mornings avoid the snooze button.

  It may seem a good idea at the time to roll over and hit the snooze button as soon as the alarm goes off — just to give yourself another ten minutes or so — but is it really doing you any good? The evidence suggest not. In actual fact you are simply robbing yourself of valuable sleep. The extra ten to twenty minutes dozing isn't actually doing you any good, and it certainly doesn't make you feel more refreshed in the mornings. You may even feel more sluggish for doing this. Shun the temptation to hit the snooze button and set your alarm later to reclaim these valuable minutes sleeping.

The table below lists the most common principles of sleep hygiene.

Basic Principles of Sleep Hygiene
Sleeping environment
Correct temperature (ideally around 17°C)
Darkened, quiet room
Comfortable bed, mattress, pillow, duvet or sheets
Non-stimulating (no computer, television, etc.)
Turn alarm clocks around so you can't see the display (this only encourages clock watching and anxiety)
Encourage
Regular bedtime routines with consistent sleep and wake times
Avoid
Working late in the evening
Excessive or late napping during the day
Falling asleep during the evening
Overstimulation near to bedtime
Exercising too late in the evening
Caffeine-containing drinks and food in the late afternoon/early evening
Large meals late at night
Checking mobile phones/emails
Bright lights before bed – and this includes the lights from phones

A final tip from a fast-food tycoon

Here's an example of a thought-control strategy developed and utilised by Ray Kroc[2] to aid sleep onset. Ray Kroc was an American entrepreneur who is probably best known for his work on revolutionising the food industry by developing systems of automation for the delivery of fast food. In the 1950s Kroc met the McDonald brothers and persuaded them to let him franchise the McDonald's name. The rest is history. Ray realised early on that good sleep was essential in order for him to perform efficiently and give 100 per cent every day: being in the restaurant business, he needed to be fresh and jovial for his customers. One of his first maxims was not to let things worry him too much and he chose to allow himself only to worry about one issue at a time, and not to fret about a problem, no matter how important it seemed. He also realised he needed to switch off his nervous tension, and in particular those anxious nocturnal thoughts that often plague us when we are trying to get to sleep. We have all experienced these at some time or another, those thoughts about a work issue that go around and around in our head.

After reading and a certain amount of self-examination, and by trial and error, Ray stumbled on a technique that worked for him. He would picture his mind as a blackboard, full of notes and ideas about things that needed doing. His trick when trying to fall asleep was to visually imagine himself cleaning the blackboard and wiping away every message and note. By doing so his mind would become completely blank. If a message came back he would simply scrub it out again. While doing so he also learnt to let his body relax fully, starting around the back of his neck, continuing slowly down through his shoulders, arms, hips, legs, etc., until he got to the tips of his toes.

Breaking this strategy down, there appear to be three distinct elements. Firstly, he was able to concentrate on one issue/worry at a time; secondly, he learnt to observe but not act on unwanted thoughts; and thirdly, he could relax at will. In essence he had developed his own version of the mindfulness discussed in chapter 14.

If you find your sleeping is still poor even though you have followed these techniques, please consult your local health professional or general practitioner.

28
Review and taking stock

'Success is not final, failure is not fatal:
it is the courage to continue that counts'

Winston Churchill

Hopefully by reading this book you have changed your core beliefs about work. You now know that you don't have to work yourself or your subordinates into the ground in order to be successful. Engaged workers are more successful, happier and more productive than overcommitted workers. However, you now need to commit yourself to developing and maintaining the lifestyle that allows you to be able both to switch off and detach from work, and at the same time allows you to be productive and creative in your working life and therefore 'still get more done'. Work hard and work smart, but also be smart in your downtime. In order to do this you need to develop the necessary discipline, and commit yourself to the lifestyle you desire, and only you can do this, not your partner or boss; you need to become your own manager. You also need to monitor your behaviour and feelings on a regular basis to ensure that you can maintain the lifestyle you have created. Work has a nasty habit of drawing us in and taking over our lives. If we let it, work *becomes* our life. Therefore in order to prevent work taking over completely we need to monitor ourselves and examine our work patterns from time to time. If you find yourself slipping back into old unwanted ways you need to take the necessary steps before things get out of hand. Of course this requires action and discipline.

See your behaviour as a traffic light

A good way to take stock is to see your life as a visual representation. When we see a visual representation of our behaviour on paper it is easier to recognise if we need to take action or not. Look at the table on the next page, and consider your life over the previous two weeks. Rate each of the three areas of (1) work, (2) health and wellbeing, and (3) lifestyle and leisure, by circling 'Yes' or 'No' in response to each statement. It is important that you are honest with yourself.

Work

1. I worked more hours than I really wanted to	Yes	No
2. In order to complete my work I let my standards slip	Yes	No
3. I started to become a perfectionist	Yes	No
4. Work started to get on top of me	Yes	No
5. I didn't speak to colleagues as much as I normally would	Yes	No
6. I have not been looking forward to going to work	Yes	No
7. I have not had enough time to clear my workstation/desk	Yes	No
8. I worked through my lunch more than once a week	Yes	No
9. I have started to become more impatient with people	Yes	No
10. I have started to miss or become late with my task, project or goals	Yes	No
Total		

Health and wellbeing

1. I felt more tired/fatigued than usual	Yes	No
2. I experienced problems getting to sleep	Yes	No
3. I found myself waking up earlier than I have planned	Yes	No
4. I didn't feel refreshed on awakening	Yes	No
5. I didn't want to get out of bed in the mornings	Yes	No
6. I felt that I was coming down with a cold or illness	Yes	No
7. I wasn't sticking to my normal eating habits	Yes	No
8. I found myself drinking alcohol more than usual	Yes	No
9. I found myself becoming more irritable with my family/friends	Yes	No
10. I became more restless than usual	Yes	No
Total		

Lifestyle and leisure

1.	I didn't spend enough time on my hobbies	Yes	No
2.	I didn't have enough time to be with family or friends	Yes	No
3.	I found it difficult to relax during my leisure time	Yes	No
4.	I did not have any clear days away from work/work issues	Yes	No
5.	I found it difficult to switch off and unwind from work	Yes	No
6.	I found it more difficult to concentrate than usual	Yes	No
7.	I felt my leisure time just slipping away	Yes	No
8.	I didn't find I enjoyed my free time	Yes	No
9.	I didn't have the energy to pursue my normal hobbies	Yes	No
10.	I was more irritable with my partner/family or friends	Yes	No

Total _____

Next, add up the number of times you circled 'Yes' for each of the three life domains. By doing the exercise you will clearly see if you are being pulled too much to work issues. I like to think of this exercise as a warning system using the traffic light analogy. Green is good, so proceed as usual. Amber is a warning that you need to do something about your work habits as you are at an increased risk of becoming chronically fatigued or ill, and red is the warning light telling you that you need to take immediate action. If you see yourself being drawn into the amber and red areas you can read through the suggested chapters again. I would, however, recommend you to read the whole book again as often we see things the second time around we skipped over on first reading. Also, a second reading reinforces the message. However, it is important to remember that this is not a diagnostic tool but an indicator that you are increasing your risk of slipping back into old habits, and a gentle warning that your health could be affected long term if you do not change your behaviour.

	Work	Health and wellbeing	Lifestyle and leisure
Red	6–10		
Amber	1–5		
Green	0		

Slipping back into old habits

One of the biggest challenges to changing any health behaviour, be it getting fit, following a healthy diet or following the instructions and advice in a self-help book, is to keep practising and keep following the principles of the programme. Obstacles will invariably come along, and you will find the going gets tough at times. There will be times when you will find it difficult not to become distracted from your goal. Don't be too discouraged if you find yourself occasionally slipping back into old habits. Actually, habits, once formed, become embedded in our conscience and are particularly hard to break. Once you have mastered the techniques in this book, your new approach to work will eventually become a habit.

People who go on food diets don't expect to suddenly reach their target weight the next day. Losing weight correctly takes time, patience and a lot of willpower. Similarly, learning to change the way you think and approach work will take time. Changing any behaviour in order to form a new habit takes time. Learning how to balance the demands of work and personal life will, inevitably, take time. There is no magic switch you can flick to instantly transfer you from work mode to 'me' mode; if there were, life would be less rich, less rewarding and there would be no need for a book like this. When you are really busy it is difficult to think clearly, but try to find the space to take time out, to think about the things that are important to you. If it helps, you could even set a time in your calendar to remind you to do this. In the early days you could schedule an appointment more often and then reduce this to every three months or so, just to keep you on track.

Allow yourself time

As stated earlier in this book, you wouldn't expect to run a marathon with only a couple of weeks of preparatory jogging, or swim the Channel without first learning to swim. Likewise, you cannot expect to switch from being a work-centred individual to a more rounded figure without doing the necessary training and following the exercises. You need to persist and show dedication. Keep focusing on your goal, but not obsessively. There will be times when you are simply too busy and you will have to devote more time than usual to work. We all experience busy times when we feel compelled to put the extra hours in. When this happens, don't worry, just accept it, work through it and get the work completed. Once this hurdle has been cleared go back to how you were. Normally things will balance out as work demands tend to come in cycles. The trick is to know when your attention is being directed too much or for too long to work matters above other areas of your life. This is why it is important to plan breaks and spend time away to allow yourself to rewind and reflect.

Use the measure reported in chapter 5 to monitor your progress over time

You should by now be aware of, and hopefully have practised, a number of different recovery strategies, and I suspect that you have found your favourites. You will have also found when and where some methods work better. The key is not to become over-reliant on one particular method. For example, having a massage is for most people a very good way of relaxing and unwinding following a busy day. However, a poor strategy would be to have a massage every day. It is good to keep practising different techniques. It may be possible for you to discover what you believe to be the 'best recovery' method — I have my personal favourites — but it may not be possible for one reason or another for you to initiate that particular recovery method at that particular moment. It is therefore important that you are able to equip yourself with an armoury of different strategies. From time to time, it will be good practice to go back over the exercise chapters in the book.

As I said above, there is no one formula that fits all. You will need to decide which techniques and strategies work best for you. Over the years we have conducted workshops and presentations to literally hundreds of people, and not one person has not found some techniques useful. I have also received many testimonials from people who have followed the programme and been amazed by the changes they have seen in themselves.

When the going gets tough

Behind every successful man or woman you will find a series of failures. You need to accept initial failures as only minor setbacks along the road to your destination. There is a saying that people don't fail, they just simply stop trying. You don't fail as a person, but your behaviour may fail you now and then. When it does, you just have to dust yourself down and keep moving, sometimes to the left, sometimes to the right, but never backwards. Take responsibility for your life, and keep moving forwards.

In almost any self-help book — I prefer the term self-education — there will inevitably be a section on accepting responsibility. You need to accept responsibility for what you do and what happens to you in order to take control of your life. It is easy when things don't go well to blame fate, bad luck or other people. You may have heard people say, 'I'm just too busy to do these exercises', 'It was not meant to happen'. This may be partially true, but you need to wise up. Every successful person has experienced setbacks along the way. What sets these people apart is that they never give up. Most people read through a self-help book and then put it down and go on their merry way. Ultimately life is about choice. You often hear people say they would like more choice, more freedom, but freedom and choice involve responsibility and most people who don't succeed at anything (albeit diets, exercise programmes) are frightened of responsibility! 'It is not my fault I put on weight, it is my job.' It is always someone else's fault. Having the ability to choose, we think is a right but maybe we should consider it a gift. In this book I have provided you with information and it is up to you to decide how to use this information.

Be realistic – not all thinking about work is bad

As you hopefully have discovered by reading this book, not only is working too many hours bad for us in the long term, continually thinking about work issues when not at work is equally as bad, if not even worse, for us. There are many things tempting us to work or think about work during our leisure. Working long hours is good for the economy. The more money we earn the more we can spend on leisure goods, this results in more employment and more tax for the government. However, this also comes at a cost that creeps up on us. Unfortunately this can become a vicious circle, as the more we spend on consumer products, holidays or coffee, the harder we have to work to continue our lifestyle. As a society we are always encouraged to be more productive, etc., but there comes a point where we simply have to slow down and find time for ourselves.

By now, you should have realised that it also doesn't matter whether you think about work outside your normal contractual hours. As stated throughout the book, I don't think it is possible or even desirable to completely switch off from work. Those people who say they leave work behind as soon as they leave the office or place of work are, in my opinion, either lying or they never really switched on to work in the first place. We should be aiming to improve all aspects of our life. Like it or not, work takes much of our time, and we should try to make it as rewarding and as interesting as possible. If you therefore find yourself thinking about an issue outside of work, this is not only acceptable, it is also normal. It is completely rational to think about issues at work when you are not at work, and many good ideas pop into our heads when we least expect them.

Many good ideas and inventions often result from a sudden flash of insight, and these invariably appear when least expected. Finding a new solution to work problems outside our actual working hours can give us pleasure and be quite rewarding. Sometimes a thought or idea tries to form in our mind but takes a while for it to completely take shape. It percolates in our deepest recesses, and when it is ready it will appear in our consciousness. This could be at any time during the day, evening or even during the night. If I have to prepare a talk I often find it helps to mull it over in my head for a few weeks prior to the talk itself. Something I watch on television, or have read, will trigger a thought that I can work on and incorporate into my talk. Or it may be something someone said in a conversation totally irrelevant to the topic of my talk that will trigger a thought that I can use. Work and home life therefore should not be completely bound. Also, society would be less technologically advanced if we stopped thinking about work issues as soon as we left work. So don't cut work off completely in your free time. Simply try not to be so emotionally fixated on work. We need to be rational about this, and common sense suggests that the line between work and home and home and work should be slightly blurred.

What is the ideal day?

What is the perfect day? Ideally, we would spend one third of the day working, one third on leisure pursuits and the remaining in a relaxed state of sleep. We would wake up feeling refreshed, take a shower or bath, followed by a healthy, leisurely breakfast, and then travel to work energised and ready to engage in the tasks that await. Work is not too far from our home but far enough away that we don't keep bumping into work colleagues during our free time. During a productive working day we would have at least fifteen to twenty minutes' break in the morning and a similar break in the afternoon, where we can sit down away from our workstation and chat to colleagues or just sit quietly. An hour for a leisurely but light lunch consisting of a bowl of soup or piece of fish or chicken with salad or vegetables. Possibly taking a little walk either before or after eating. On finishing work, the workstation or desk is tidied, awaiting your return the following day. You are happy as work has been rewarding and satisfying. During the commute home, mobile devices would be switched off or used to play recreational games or for listening to music, and/or we would simple relax and reflect on the day. If travelling by car it may be nice, if the opportunity arises, to pull over and have a coffee or a quiet stroll in a preferred place. On the commute home, we would be mindful and pay full attention to our surroundings. On arriving home you would get changed, have a shower or relaxing bath if needed, and then spend a few minutes talking to your partner or children. You would find some time just to be by yourself in your favourite chair or spot in the garden, maybe with a tea or coffee, taking a few moments to reflect, to ponder, to just be. Work is finished for the day so there's no need to think about it any more. If a good idea or solution to a work-related issue happens to pop into your head, note it down, so you can deal with it tomorrow and then park it. Following a light, relaxing dinner, possibly with a glass of something, you would go out for the evening with your partner or friends, or spend your time pursuing your favourite hobby or self-growth activities. You enjoy this time, and you firmly believe you are not missing out by not working. You know that top employees tend to expose themselves to experiences outside of work, which they can apply and utilise in their work. Then it would be early to bed for a full eight hours' sleep.

If only it was this easy! As far as I can tell for most of us who live in the real world, this ideal is not possible. We all have our own individual needs and life circumstances to attend, and many of us are lives conjurors, constant juggling work, projects, partners, children, parents, grandparents, pets, etc. And these needs vary across time, sometimes with little warning. Life is really about compromise and negotiation. We need to attend to certain things but we also need to spend time on our needs, without feeling guilty. It is not possible to have complete control and if it were life would become predictable and boring. So manage your work and home life, but don't become anxious if things don't always go to plan.

Prevention plans

The bottom line is that any behaviour that is good or bad can be broken. People do it all the time; for example, they start or stop smoking, start or stop exercising, start or stop dieting. The tricky part is not initiating a new behaviour, but sticking with the new behaviour until it becomes a habit. Once a behaviour becomes habitual it is hard to break as it will become part of your psychological make-up. You have taken the first step by recognising the need to change, and the second step by learning how to unwind after work. The next step involves adhering to your plan. Remember, perfection is never attainable, and therefore a 'perfect' life is neither the ideal nor our goal. Knowing when to push but also knowing when to back off is a judgement call. If you can find this middle ground you will strike the right balance between being both productive/creative but also giving yourself time to relax and enjoy the fruits of your labour.

Good luck!

Notes

Chapter 1: All work and no play

1. Sokejima and Kagamimori (1998). 'Working hours as a risk factor for acute myocardial infarction in Japan: case-control study', *BMJ*, 19, 317,775 – 80.

Chapter 2: Why should you learn to switch off?

1. Gallie, D., White, M., Cheng, Y., and Tomlinson, M. (1998). *Restructuring the Employment Relationship*. Oxford: Oxford University Press.

2. Felstead, A., Gallie, D., and Green, F. (2002). *Work Skills in Britain 1986–2001*. Nottingham: DfES Publications.

3. Suadicani, P., Hein, H. O., and Gyntelberg, F. (1993). 'Are Social Inequalities as Associated with the Risk of Ischemic-Heart-Disease a Result of Psychosocial Working-Conditions?', *Atherosclerosis*, 101(2), 165 – 75.

4. Kivimaki, M., Leino-Arjas, P., Kaila-Langas, L., Luukkonen, R., Vahtera, J., Elovainio, M., Härmä, M., and Kirjonen, J. (2006). 'Is incomplete recovery from work a risk marker of cardiovascular death? Prospective evidence from industrial employees, *Psychosomatic Medicine*, 68(3), 402 – 7.

Chapter 3: Are you overworked?

1. Cropley, M., Rydstedt, L. W., Devereux, J. J., and Middleton, B. (2013). 'The Relationship between Work-related Rumination and Evening and Morning Salivary Cortisol Secretion. Stress and Health', DOI: 10.1002/smi.2538.
2. Cropley, M., Michalianou, G., Pravettoni, G., and Millward, L. (2012), 'The relation of post work ruminative thinking with eating behaviour', *Stress and Health*, 28, 23−30, DOI: 10.1002/smi.1397.

Chapter 4: Why your boss should be interested in unwinding

1. Organ, D. W. (1988). *Organizational Citizenship Behavior: The Good Soldier Syndrome*. Lexington, MA: Lexington Books.

Chapter 10: Distract your mind and fill the void

1. Steptoe, A., Lundwall, K., and Cropley, M. (2000). 'Gender, family structure and cardiovascular activity during the working day and evening', *Social Science and Medicine*, 50, 531−9.
2. Vanderkam, Laura (2013-01-17). *What the Most Successful People Do on the Weekend* (Kindle Locations 69−70). Penguin Books, Kindle edition.

Chapter 11: Develop a hobby

1. Uusiautti, Satu, and Määttä, Kaarina (2011). 'The Process of Becoming a Top Worker', *International Education Studies*, 4, November 2011.
2. Schwartz, D. J. (1979). *The Magic of Thinking Big*. London: Pocket Books.

Chapter 12: Leave work at home

1. Cropley, M., and Millward, L. J. (2009). 'How do individuals "switch-off" from work during leisure? A qualitative description of the unwinding process in high and low ruminators', *Leisure Studies*, 28, 333−47.

Chapter 19: Vacations and mini breaks

1. Nawijn, J., Marchand, M. A., Veenhoven, R., and Vingerhoets, A. J. (2010). 'Vacationers happier, but most not happier after a holiday', *Applied Research Quality Life*, 5, 35–47.

Chapter 20: Make breaks count

1. Fritz, C., Lam, C. F., and Spreitzer, G. M. (2011). 'It's the Little Things That Matter: An Examination of Knowledge Workers' Energy Management', *Academy of Management Perspectives*, 28–39.

Chapter 24: Friends and colleagues

1. Berkman, L. F., and Syme, S. L. (1979). 'Social networks, host resistance, and mortality: a nine-year follow-up study of Alameda County residents', *American Journal of Epidemiology*, 109, 186–204.
2. Undén, A-L, Orth-Gomér, K., and Elofsson, S. (1991). 'Cardiovascular effects of social support in the work place: Twenty-four-hour ECG monitoring of men and women', *Psychosomatic Medicine*, 53, 50–60.

Chapter 26: Physical health

1. Lee, C. D., Blair, S. N., and Jackson, A. S. (1999). 'Cardiorespiratory fitness, body composition, and all-cause and cardiovascular disease mortality in men', *American Journal of Clinical Nutrition*, 69, 373–80.

Chapter 27: Sleep

1. Landolt, H. P., Dijk, D. J., Gaus, S. E., and Borbely, A. A. (1995). 'Caffeine reduces low-frequency delta activity in the human sleep EEG', *Neuropsychopharmacology*, 12, 229–38.
2. Kroc, R. (1977). *Grinding It Out: The Making of McDonald's*. New York: St Martin's Paperbacks.

index